Evening Standard

101

THINGS
You Need To
KNOW
ABOUT
WINE

ANDREW JEFFORD

SIMON & SCHUSTER

A VIACOM COMPANY

For Charlie and Jimmy Jefford: tomorrow's drinkers

First published in Great Britain by Simon & Schuster UK Ltd, 1998
A Viacom Company

1 3 5 7 9 10 8 6 4 2

Simon & Schuster UK Ltd
Africa House
64-78 Kingsway
London WC2B 6AH

Simon & Schuster Australia
Sydney

Cover design: Neal Cobourne
Text design: Moore Lowenhoff
Typeset by Stylize Digital Artwork
Printed and bound in Italy

A CIP catalogue record for this book is available from the
British Library

ISBN 0-671-02202-4

Contents

Part 2: The Winery: Making Wine

Part 3: The Cellar: Ageing Wine

Part 4: The Glass: Tasting Wine

Part 5: The Shop: Buying Wine

Part 6: The Table: Serving Wine

Introduction

Wine is fun.

You could just leave it at that. Just settle – why not? – for buying the occasional recommendation, drinking what comes along, enjoying the flavours, binning the names, recycling the bottles. Who wants to be a wine bore?

Unless you make a living out of wine, you don't need to know anything about it. All you need to decide is whether you fancy a red or a white, and how much you want to pay for it. 101 things? Forget it. Leave this book on the shelf.

But then again ... maybe once in a while you taste something which is not just delicious, but startlingly so. Suddenly you can't stop sipping; suddenly the wine ceases to be simply an alcoholic drink and becomes a sort of liquid umbilical cord, connecting you to the past, to another country, to a different way of life, to a pleasure more profound than you ever thought you could find in a glass. Suddenly you understand why wine and passion go together; suddenly you do want to know more. This book is for that moment.

Wines are very like people: no two are alike. Any book which claimed to tell you 'everything you need to know' about wine would be as surely doomed to failure as one which claimed to tell you everything you need to know about human psychology. So let's avoid misunderstandings; let me briefly describe what this book will not tell you.

Earth, water, air, fire: these were the four elements anciently thought to constitute the universe, and which continue to play a role in our symbolic thinking, even if the physics has moved on a bit. You could, following the same pleasingly neat lines, say that four elements define the quality and flavour of any wine. Earth would be the place in which the grapes are grown. Water would equate with the vintage – all the weather, in other words, which the vine had to endure between the first buds swelling on the wood in the still depths of winter and its grapes being snipped off wizening stalks in early autumn sunshine. Air would be its genetic inheritance – the particular type or variety of grape or grapes from which a wine is made. And fire is the human element: the man or woman who said "OK: let's pick tomorrow morning at five"; who oversaw fermentation; who decided if and when to run the wine into an oak barrel, through a filter, into a bottle.

What I am going to try to do is to tell you about these four elements (regions, viticulture, grape varieties and winemaking) in general. But not in particular: no lists of recommended producers, no endless château names or bin numbers, no detailed discussion of who botched the 1997 vintage in Bordeaux or of who's producing the best Shiraz nowadays in the Barossa. If you want that kind of nitty-gritty, read newspaper wine columns or buy some of the guide books I recommend on page 232. What I'm aiming to provide is what the French call a *tour d'horizon* – a 'journey around the horizon'. I hope the journey, like wine itself, will be fun; I hope that, by the end, you'll have a clearer idea of the lie of the land, and feel confident enough to do a little exploring on your own.

Ready, then? Let's go.

Part 1

The Vineyard: Growing Wine

1 Vineyards are unique

And as we gather speed, consider this.

There are no pork writers. How many fish columns are there in the weekend newspapers? I've never seen a section in a bookshop devoted to the ice-cream industry; no one, to my knowledge, has yet made a tv series in which great potato growers of the world are interviewed and profiled.

The comparisons are not as far-fetched as they might seem. Every bottle in the largest supermarket, bottle store or cellar you've ever been into is made from one primary ingredient alone: fresh grapes. No other single agricultural product has so much discussion, enthusiasm and passion lavished upon it. Grapes, when turned into wine, provide work for peaceful armies of human beings in most non-Moslem countries of the world. It's not just down to alcohol, either: half a dozen men could produce enough vodka to keep a capital city rolling drunk from one year's end to the next, but vodka doesn't evoke one-twentieth of the respect and interest which wine does. Why is wine so special?

The answer is that wine is the most expressive and memorable way in which human beings can taste geography, can taste places on earth, can taste the world.

A piece of plain pork tastes much the same whether the pig from which it was cut grew fat in Buffalo or Bolton. Squid from the South China Sea and from the Mediterranean is not hugely different when sliced, slashed and fried. A Gala apple grown in New Zealand might be slightly crisper and less sweet than one from Washington State, but there's only a notch or two in it. Yet when one man in Burgundy makes two wines in exactly the same way from vineyards a few hundred yards apart, the difference can be remarkable. The first wine (which is called Chassagne-Montrachet and sells for £15 a bottle) makes a pleasant, gently nutty glass at five years old and is turning dull at ten; the second wine (which is called Le Montrachet and sells for £100 a bottle) is still rather hard and inarticulate at five years old but at twenty smells of cream and wild mushrooms, flowers, toasted brioche and toasted hazelnuts, and tastes more sumptuously gratifying and dryly rich than you would think possible. You can, truly, taste the difference between two wines made from grapes grown in vineyards five minutes' from each other. The soil is different, a stonier and purer limestone; the vineyard sits a little higher on the hillside, and the sun creeps on to it earlier after dawn and is still lingering there while the men and women of the village are eating their dinners; the cool air at night slides past it and down to the road and the valley bottom; passing showers of rain or hail have a habit of chosing other targets. Grapes are the litmus test by which such things become apparent to our noses, to our taste buds. Glass in one hand, corkscrew in the other, seated at your kitchen table, you can travel the world.

That is why vineyards are unique.

2 Vines want to climb trees

Vines are, in plant terms, agile weaklings. You could call them the hitch-hikers of the tree world. In their natural environment – a thick forest, say, somewhere in Central Asia one or two million years ago – they would seek the light of the canopy by clambering twenty or thirty feet in the air through the luminous green tangle, grasping trunks and branches firmly enough to defeat even high winds with their coiling tendril fingers. Grapes dangled temptingly for birds who ensured, after a sweet and pippy meal, the vine's dispersal.

The *first winegrowers* were probably forest goatherds around 7,000 years ago in present-day *Georgia* or *Armenia*, living in clearings where they could keep the vines in light, and more systematically fruitful, at lower levels. If you travel in rural *Italy* or *Portugal* today, you may still see vines casually trained against trees. Many of the greatest artistic depictions of the vine, moreover, explore its nature as a climber. There is a shallow Greek drinking cup in a museum in Munich worked by one of the black-figure masters, Exekias, which shows *Dionysus* crossing the sea. Dolphins leap about the boat in which the bearded, crowned god is reclining, while up above his neatly-trimmed sail spreads a vine-like heaventree bearing heavy clusters of grapes. Beauty, comfort, solace, even shelter: the core of the vine's appeal.

You don't really need to know any of this, though it does explain why vineyards look like they do. Since vines enjoy climbing, most winegrowers provide something for them to climb on: posts linked by wires, called a *trellis*. Exactly how the vines are trained on the trellis is crucial, and much research in the 1990s has been aimed at understanding the optimum exposure of both leaves and grapes to available *sunlight*. The fact that vines are climbers, too, explains the necessity for a severe winter *pruning*, and usually a trim or two over the summer months.

Vines can, if pruned severely enough, grow unsupported by a trellis: the stumpy black claws rising up out of the cold, hard ground which form such a distinctive feature of the Mediterranean landscape in winter are called 'goblet' or *bush vines*. Indeed you'll sometimes see the term 'bush vine' on wine labels from countries like *South Africa* and

Australia, vaguely promising some sort of superiority of flavour. The promise is based on the logic that bush vines are nearly always old vines (they're very hard work to prune and harvest, so only fanatical traditionalists would plant them today), and old vines are thought to make better wine than young vines. As usual, there are two schools of thought as to why this might be so: Europeans tend to claim it's because old vines are more deeply rooted, giving them greater soil and mineral exposure; Australians are more likely to say it's simply because old vines are weak and do not, therefore, overproduce either vegetation or fruit, as young vigorous vines tend to. The same effects, they'd claim, can be achieved by the correct pruning and training of younger vines.

3
Vines are two plants in one

Meet a terrifying creature.

It has a fat, yellow, shield-shaped body with two beady little eyes. A brace of feelers protruding from its headpart resemble small crab claws. Sometimes it grows six strangely articulated legs; very occasionally it even grows lacy, sweeping wings. Mostly it just sits around in a mess of eggs and gobbles root sap. How big is it? Oh, about the size of a pinhead. And it nearly wiped out the world's vineyards.

Phylloxera devastatrix is its ringing, horror-movie name; botanists now call it *Dactylasphaera vitifoliae*. Because of its existence, its cunning life cycle and its formidable appetite, most of the world's vines are now two plants in one. Above ground, the plants (or scions) belong to the *Vitis vinifera* species. At ground level, there is a graft; below ground, the roots generally belong to another Vitis species altogether, or a Vitis hybrid.

Our fat little bug cruised, shipboard, from its native America to Europe in the middle of the nineteenth century on botanical specimens. American *Vitis* species had become resistant, in that nifty evolutionary way, to its depradations; *Vitis vinifera*, the species from which all wine (most of it European) was then made, was vulnerable. The disaster which followed is hard for us to imagine: almost twenty years of sick and dying vineyards across Europe. Endless ruined livelihoods; endless lost pleasure. Grafting European *Vitis vinifera* on to rootstocks derived from American native vines has proved a durable solution, though there was a recent hiccup when (ironically enough) many of California's vineyards were mown down – due to inadequate hybrid rootstocks and a feisty new phylloxera biotype.

Why do you need to know this? Partly because 'phylloxera' is one of those terms wine enthusiasts love to bandy about, but partly because you may come across back labels on bottles proclaiming the wine within is made from the fruit of ungrafted vines (sometimes called 'national' vines). Some small areas of Europe (especially where vineyards are grown in sand, which the little fat one hates), some large areas in Australia, and almost all of Chile and Argentina have never suffered phylloxera attack.

Is the wine better as a consequence? No. Most of the greatest wines in the world today are made from the fruit of grafted vines. Eat sand, louse: you lost.

4
The vine has many varieties

Suppose you and I were to find ourselves sitting next to each other on a long train journey. And suppose (this is not, alas, to strain credulity) the train was to break down. Boredom would set in; we'd get talking;

I'd learn what you do for a living, and you'd discover my job, too. "I don't know much about wine," you'd tell me, "but I like it." We'd talk about wine, and I'd discover that, despite what you said, you do know quite a lot. You'd tell me what sort of Chardonnays you liked, and whether, perhaps, you preferred wines based on Cabernet Sauvignon to those made from Pinot Noir.

It hasn't always been like this, but for most wine-drinkers nowadays, a knowledge of grape varieties is by far the easiest route to understanding wine.

As we learned in the last section, almost all vines (above ground) belong to the *Vitis vinifera* species. This species is subdivided into tens of thousands of distinct varieties, each of which will have a unique appearance in the vineyard, and flavour in the glass.

Tens of thousands? Help!

Don't panic. Around twenty or thirty varieties are the winners, accounting for well over half of all the wine we drink. Another fifty varieties, let's say, would have something or other going for them which makes them of commercial use, though as a consumer you don't really need to know much about them. And the rest are of interest only to ampelographers – botanists specialising in vines. If you can fix in your mind, and your mouth, the character of those twenty or thirty winner-varieties, you'll be at least half-way towards a comprehensive understanding of wine. Not too difficult, is it?

But why, you might ask, does getting a handle on grape varieties only take you half way? Two reasons. The first is that many wines (and, some people believe, the greatest wines) are made from a blend of varieties rather than a single variety.

Secondly, the most interesting wines are made in such a way as to taste not only of a variety but also of a place on earth. "A Cabernet Sauvignon from

Bordeaux bears a much closer resemblance to a Merlot from Bordeaux than it does to a Cabernet Sauvignon from Australia or Chile," said the late Peter Sichel of Château Palmer, quite accurately. So for a comprehensive understanding of wine, you also need to tackle the issues of blends and of regions. Since many blends are part of regional traditions, the two go together to some extent. We'll be exploring both grape varieties and regions systematically in Section Five, the heavy-duty section, of this book. For the time being, all you need to remember is that most wine is made from a limited number of famous grape varieties, such as Chardonnay, Cabernet Sauvignon or Pinot Noir.

One last thing, before we leave this subject for the time being. A grape variety planted in a traditional vineyard resembles, if you like, a human family: its vines are similar enough one to another to be recognizable, but they are far from being genetically identical. For that, you need a single clone of a particular variety, such as the Pommard clone of Pinot Noir (widely planted in California, Chile and South Africa). Much effort in twentieth-century viticulture has gone into clonal selection, but as with most attempts to improve nature this has brought both advantages and disadvantages. The main advantage is that you can fill your vineyard with healthy and (should you wish) high-yielding vines; the main disadvantage is that wine produced exclusively from a single clone often tastes boring and monotonous.

The opposite of clonal selection is mass or massal selection, where vines are propagated from the healthiest and best-performing vines in a genetically heterogenous population, such as might be found in a traditional Pinot Noir vineyard in Burgundy itself. Most winegrowers nowadays believe massal selection is essential for nuanced wines.

5 Vines have deep roots

Almost ten years ago, on my first serious research visit (or, depending on your point of view, free jaunt) to a vineyard region, I got up before everyone else to walk around the vineyards and take photographs. Behind the house was a new vineyard, built on a terrace which had been, quite literally, blasted out of the rock. It was only eight in the morning, yet the heat was already searing my neck as I walked from tiny vine to tiny vine.

After a few shots, I gave up. I laid the camera to one side and simply stared at those little plants in amazement. How were they going to survive? Under such a sun, in bare rock, without irrigation? How were they going to last out the day to come, let alone a whole season? Suddenly they seemed to symbolise life itself, fragile almost to the point of hopelessness, yet tenacious and ultimately (the evidence was in the vineyards soaring about me) triumphant.

This was Portugal's Douro Valley, where port is made. Soil is a rarity in the Douro's vineyards; mostly they are sited in boulder-fields and rock-yards. The rock is schist – porous and cleaving, almost soft to the touch. The schist holds reserves of winter rain within it like water in a mineral sponge; baby vines can survive because their roots swiftly penetrate down into the rock and find that water. The roots of an adult vine under such conditions routinely descend 20 metres (66 feet); Rhône valley winegrower Michel Chapoutier claims the roots of very old vines may even descend as far as 140 metres (460 feet) within favourable rock formations. A vine is a midget above ground, and a giant below it.

The Douro's vines are by no means alone in growing in stony, near-sterile environments. The very finest Bordeaux wines come from vines which paddle in gravel; Germany's greatest Rieslings lurch out of a steep rubble of slate; some Châteauneuf-du-Pape is famously rooted amid giant glacier-rolled puddingstones, while some of the newer vineyards in New Zealand's Marlborough region have been planted in pure river-bed pebbles. Growers in all these regions believe that the effort that their vines put into thrusting deeper into the rock improves the quality of the final wine. Vines, the theory runs, like to suffer – and drinkers can taste the suffering.

Why might a thirsty, stressed vine gripping deeply into subsoil and rock produce better wine than a fat, well-nourished one basking in deep, moist soils?

One answer, the scientifically provable one, is that free-draining yet moisture-retentive subsoils are ideal for vines. Too much rain or irrigation? Moist, deep soils create a shallow root system, and waterlogged subsoils actually kill vine roots. Of course, matters can go too far the other way: drought-stricken, desiccated *subsoils* stress vines to such an extent that the plant gives up trying to reproduce (via tasty, wine-friendly grapes) and concentrates instead on its own survival. The ideal lies somewhere in the middle. Vine roots searching out moisture reserves deep in bed-rock are, in fact, not suffering but enjoying themselves. Moderate nutrition and water supply below ground help them to produce the ideal ratio of leaves to bunches of grapes above ground. The vines make the most of the available light and warmth, keep the amount of grapes produced to an optimum level, and, fill those grapes with flavour-bearing compounds.

The second, and so far scientifically unprovable, answer concerns the exposure of those roots to soil and rock minerals, and the ability of wines actually to acquire mineral or earthy flavours from the soil or rock in which the vines are growing. Here the evidence is in the glass, as it has been for hundreds of years. Tasters have always noticed that the Mosel valley's greatest Rieslings have a slaty taste, that claret from the Graves region tastes gravelly, that fine Chablis has a mineral quality to its flavour, that the greatest red wines of the southern Rhône and of Languedoc are earthy. Buy some good examples of these wines and, by the second or third bottle, you'll know exactly what I'm talking about.

Yet give the same wines to a scientist, ask him or her to boil off all the moisture and analyse what remains, and they'll not be able to show you a spoonful of slate, gravel, minerals or earth. We mistrust mystery and try to exclude it from our lives, thereby disfiguring and improverishing the human experience. Wine, though, has a mysterious side to its character. Its ability to lift out dark profundities of flavour from the earth is an example of this. No one knows why wines sometimes seem to taste of the soil in which they grew – but they do.

6 Vines like heat

Few of those growing up (as I did) in northern latitudes will ever forget their first sight of a vineyard. Mine came as I was gazing out from the back seat of a Rover 2000, driving south through France – an exotic and most decidedly foreign country – on a family holiday. Vineyards emphasised, agriculturally, the strangeness and otherness of this place. Not only was it a good-time crop, a crop grown under the signs of fun and naughtiness, but it was also emphatically southern, a crop the north could not support. I was used to mournful, muddy fields of sugar beet.

Why was East Anglia not full of vineyards? Heat, in a word. Vines don't wake from dormancy and begin growing until the temperature reaches 10°C (50°F); the optimum ripening temperature for grapes is around 20°C–22°C (68°F–70°F). These, of course, are averages; in many winegrowing regions, nights are much cooler than this and days much warmer. Soil temperature is also important, since warm soils stimulate plant hormones (called cytokinins) which in turn promote growth.

The converse of this is that vines hate cold weather, particularly frosts. Since vines are dormant in winter (and, by the way, they like their annual kip, which is why there are no top-quality vineyards in Florida or the Bahamas), they are relatively good at resisting winter frosts: temperatures of down to –15°C (5°F) do not generally cause problems. They detest spring frosts, though – those vicious little nips which fall on clear March or April nights after unseasonably sunny and warm days. One of the hazards of the winegrowing life is that a bad spring frost can eliminate part or all of your crop before you've even started – and with it, your annual salary. This was one reason why a number of grape varieties were usually planted in traditional European wine-growing regions. Some varieties begin growing a little later than others. If the frost takes one, the others may get away and you'll have something to eat next Christmas.

In section 23, we'll learn that varying amounts of heat from vintage to vintage affect the taste of wine. For now, though, it's time to put our shades on.

7 Vines like sunshine

Sunlight has become a winegrowing catchword recently. Heat used to be thought all-important; winegrowers nowadays, though, pay just as much attention to sunlight. Heat, of course, enjoys the advantage of being easy to measure, whereas gauging sunlight intensity has always been a tricky matter;

the anatomy of sunlight, too, is complicated. There is, quite literally, more to sunlight than meets the eye, since much of it is invisible to us. But in the end all heat is sunlight, as anybody who's ever broken through to the world beyond the clouds in an aeroplane will realise. All light is sunlight, too; it just falls, crucially, through different filters. It's struggling to get through the thick cloud and murky grey mist of a February morning in the northern hemisphere's higher latitudes as I type this.

How does a vine make a grape? With sunshine, chiefly. Using the sun's energy (which we perceive as heat) it turns carbon dioxide in the atmosphere into sugar. It does this in its leaves, by what's called photosynthesis. The sugar then moves from the leaves down into the fruit; the roots contribute water (to make juice), minerals and trace elements. Hey presto: a grape.

A large part of the challenge of growing the best grapes possible, therefore, is connected with helping your vine to make ideal use of the sunlight available to it. Vines, like humans, can soak up too much light and become burned, but in general their tolerance is much higher than ours. Fair-skinned vineyard workers in parts of the southern hemisphere where ultra-violet radiation is very high quickly discover this to their cost. I've stood looking at vineyards in New Zealand's Marlborough region squinting despite my sunglasses, amazed at the vines' green contentment under what seemed to me a Niagara of silvery brightness. The hillside grasses were long since seared, and the fence posts bleached white.

The chief method for making the most of this sunlight is called 'canopy management'. This means training and trimming a vine's growth so as to optimise the exposure of both the leaves and the fruit to light and heat, and allow air to circulate freely within it. It's not a formula: correct canopy management for hotspots like California's San Joaquin Valley or South Australia's Riverland, where the grapes might need partial protection from the sun, differs from canopy management in Champagne or Germany's Mosel valley, where, in general, the more sunlight exposure the fruit enjoys, the better. Soil fertility, latitude, topography, moisture, wind, vineyard mechanisation – all these, too, affect your strategy. But the basic idea is to open up the hedge so that the vine can perform efficiently and healthily and the fruit ripen fully.

Over centuries, that's exactly what scrupulous winegrowers in Europe's top-quality regions have done anyway. A stroll through the immaculate, neatly trimmed vineyards of Château Margaux or Château Latour in Bordeaux shows canopy management in action. But not all vines are grown in such ideal locations, nor have so many man-hours lavished on them. One reason why Bulgaria's red wines, for example, have tasted 'greener' and more herbaceous than they should during the 1990s is that the vineyards, overdue for a return to private ownership, are badly tended and unkempt, with bunches of grapes hidden away under a mass of foliage. If there were half the number of shoots and leaves, and the bunches could breathe freely and sunbathe for much of the day, the wine would taste better.

8 Vines grow flowers

Few fruits could be more showy than a bunch of black grapes as it hangs plumply in the sunshine, both nonchalant and generous, as warm to the touch as a human hand.

By contrast few flowers could be more shy than those that parent grapes. You could walk past a

vineyard in late May or early June and not even
notice that every vine in every row was in full flower.
Save, perhaps, for the penetrating, strangely limey
smell.

Yet no flowers, no grapes. There always are
flowers, as it happens; the problem is that turbulent
weather – high wind, heavy rain – at flowering time
can cause a proportion of them to fail or abort, or for
the process to become a long-drawn-out and
inconsistent one (as in Bordeaux in 1997, when it
took a month). Flowering is very definitely a finger-
crossing moment for winegrowers. The ideal is calm,
warm weather, so that flowering can take place
swiftly and steadily (as it did in Bordeaux in 1996, in
just 12 days). Growers generally want flowering to be
as early as possible, too (once, of course, the risk of
frosts passes, which coincides in Europe with the
three 'Ice Saints' days on May 11th to 13th). In a hot
spring in low latitudes, flowering can be as little as
six weeks after budburst; out at the chilly viticultural
limits, by contrast, it can take three months or so.
My heart always bleeds for English winegrowers
waiting anxiously for their vines to flower in a cool
July, knowing that every day's delay will make full
ripening more and more difficult to achieve before
murky autumn closes in.

The vine flower is discretion itself. Before
flowering, the bunch unfolds as if it was already
spiked with little green fruits – but these 'fruits' are
in fact tight green petals wrapped back over the
flower head. When the big moment comes, the
petals unfold from the bottom outwards and then
drop off as a unit, at which point the flower looks like
a monk slipping off his cowl. The tiny yellow
stamens shed their pollen grains on to the central
part of the flower, which contains the ovary. This
central part swells up to become a grape; everything
else falls off. A little gentle breeze and vagrant

insects help the process, but aren't strictly necessary;
vine flowers can do it for themselves, as has been
proved by wrapping polythene bags around the
flower heads and ensuring their immobility.

9 Vines like hills

Throughout much of Europe, winegrowing is just
entering its third millennium. The remains of Roman
press-houses in the vineyards testify, astonishingly, to
the fact that 2,000 years ago men and women were
bent over vines in the golden sunshine of late
September, slicing bunches of grapes off their stems
with sharp hooks. German winegrower Ernie Loosen
loves to point out, as part of his outspoken campaign
against mediocre modern German wines, the Roman
press-house sited in the Erdener Prälat vineyard. It
lies ... well, at the bottom of a mountain. One false
move in the vineyards grafted into the steep slopes
and terraces above, and the hapless pruner or picker
might tumble to a bone-shattering death. The
Romans, Ernie points out, did not put their press
house in the flat lands across the river, lands which
are now covered in high-yielding, machine-harvested
vines for 'Hock' and Liebfraumilch. They put it
where they had put their vineyards. On the steepest
slopes they could find.

Vines, most students of wine quickly learn, love
a steep and open hill. Almost half the wines in
France seem to be called Côte or Côtes de
something or other – Côte-Rôtie, the Côte d'Or,
Côtes de Provence, Côtes de Duras, even (always a
favourite with English-speakers) Côtes du Brian.
And what does Côte mean? It means 'slope'. Hills,
again.

So why? Two answers, chiefly. The first is

drainage: hillside soils and subsoils are very rarely waterlogged, and, as we remember from section 5, vines hate having wet feet. But drainage happens above ground as well as below, and hills offer excellent air drainage. This is particularly handy on frosty nights: the cold air which causes the problems slides, toboggan-like, down the slopes and gathers in the valley floor.

The second answer is aspect. The further away from the equator you get, the more acute the angle occupied by the summer sun in the sky. Hills provide a natural correction for this regrettable fact, by (let's be literal-minded about this) lifting up the soil and pointing it in certain directions. If, thus, you're a German vine staring up at the sun from a steep south-facing hillside, the sun is more or less in the centre of your sky. Result: more sunshine, more heat, more ripeness.

You can, too, use hills to achieve the opposite effect if you want. The ideal, sun-gathering hills in Germany generally face south-west. But in hot Sicily, winegrowers struggle to find slightly cooler conditions in order to produce better wines. It's up to the hills again, but this time to search for north-facing slopes. And on the other side of the equatorial looking-glass, of course, these orientations are reversed. In New Zealand, the hottest slopes are north-facing, and the coolest slopes south-facing. Permutations of east and west can bring further benefits, largely based on the shape of the landmasses in question and the direction of prevailing winds. In Burgundy, for example, the most favoured vines generally point south-east; rains there tend to come from the west.

10 Vines like rivers

Fancy a glass of port? Its grapes grew dark beside
the glassy waters of the Douro. Some Hermitage,
perhaps? Down there's the Rhône, weaving its way
through the sprawl of Tain. The sundial in the
middle of the Wehlener Sonnenuhr vineyard looks
out, from its craggy station, across the Mosel; the
Rhine bargees, meanwhile, enjoy a superb view of
the great vineyards of Erbach and Rüdesheim as
they hump oil, coal and steel along Europe's watery
Rhine-Danube axis. You can't actually see the
Gironde estuary as you stand in the vineyards of
Château Latour, but the shimmering opal of the light
falling about you tells you it's not far away.

Well, you get the point. Vineyards and rivers
tend to hold hands, in Europe at least. As we
discovered in the last section, vines like hills – and
rivers create them. Indeed in most of the German
winelands, it is only rivers which succeed in creating
the sheltered hill sites which make winegrowing
possible at all so far north. The action of rivers in
laying down deposits of pebbles and gravel can also
create ideal vinegrowing soils, as in Bordeaux.

That's not all rivers do, though. Surfaces of
water reflect light in a way that a dry valley bottom
cannot, and the vines bask happily in the vertical
pool of light which results. This is perhaps most
noticeable in Switzerland, where the brilliant sun-
trap of Lake Geneva helps create some improbably
good wines. Water also helps foment mist, useful in
the production of dessert wines – see section 12 for
more on this.

Finally, a quick historical perspective. As you'll
know if you do your own shopping, wine is heavy
and cumbersome. Water is the best means of
transport for anything heavy, since much less energy

is required to move it than on land. Winegrowers in otherwise inaccessible areas stood a much better chance of selling what was, historically, a perishable product if they were able to get it quickly and swiftly on to a waiting boat.

11
Vines don't give a damn

Vines, you might be thinking by now, seem fairly choosy plants. They like slopes, they like rivers and lakes, they like well drained, stony soils with relatively low fertility. Open a wine magazine, though, and peer closely at some of the pictures of vineyards in Chile, in parts of California, in Australia or New Zealand. You may well see vineyards planted on land that's flat as a Dutch polder, where the nearest river is several hundred miles away (and where drip irrigation is a standard part of the trellis), and where the soil is rich, deep and fertile. Hey, the wines aren't too bad, either. So what is all this European claptrap?

An Australian viticultural polemicist might argue that the hills and the stony soils and the rivers of the European tradition simply create propitious conditions in high latitudes which any clever vineyard manager in a dry, hot and sunny low-latitude area can duplicate for himself. You can keep frost at bay by moving air around with windmill-like electric fans. If you have rainless summers, you can control the irrigation to duplicate, for example, a great vintage in Bordeaux (not too much water, and not too little). Soils too fertile? Simply work on your canopy to rein back vegetative growth and promote good fruit exposure, and keep yields to a reasonable level with stingy irrigation and crop thinning. What's your problem?

For ordinary, quaffing wine – no problem. Anyone who's ever enjoyed a glass of juicy Chilean Cabernet Sauvignon, whose high-yielding, irrigated, valley-floor vineyards have grown in a climate of clockwork regularity, can't really argue the case for a mediocre cheap Côtes du Rhône at the same price, no matter how hilly or stony or Europhilically-sound its vineyards. Do all the right things in the vineyard, and you can make decent wine in almost any Mediterrean-type climate.

Yet, as the Australians and Californians are busy discovering at present, great wine is not the inevitable consequence of impeccable vineyard management and vanguard winemaking. Great wines are, in the end, a gift of nature. They result when appropriate grape varieties flourish in a few very special sites (usually geologically complex and climatically favoured ones). The vines need to be husbanded intelligently and watchfully, and made into wine with solicitous restraint. That is the nearest you can come to a recipe.

Wines are, in so many ways, like human beings – an analogy I'll return to repeatedly. Here the most appropriate comparison would be with human physical beauty. Almost all of us can be ordinarily beautiful, provided we eat, sleep, exercise and dress well. Those who like us will like the way we look, and those who love us will love the way we look; the rest of the world will assess us as 'normal'. We are the quaffing wines. But there are a few human beings who are lucky enough to have been born without the thousands of imperfections which qualify our own ordinary beauty. There is a remarkable consensus about those people who are outstandingly beautiful, the Helens over which Trojan wars have been fought; it is evident, too, that this beauty is given, not acquired (it has nothing to do with plastic surgery, steroids or silicone). They are the great wines.

Life is unjust but diverse.

12
Mouldy grapes can be good grapes

We'll be taking a closer look at grapes in 'Part Two: The Winery', from section 15 onwards. What's worth noting here is that the basic instruction for most vineyard managers is to produce a smallish crop of healthy, fully ripe grapes. Since a vineyard is open to the elements, and since the natural world is full of tiny creatures in search of a free lunch and somewhere to raise a modest family of a few hundred thousand children, and since the natural world is also full of drifting airborne mushrooms looking for somewhere suitable to found a mushroomy city, and since vines and grapes are of consuming interest to viruses, spiders, moths, badgers, wild boar and parrots (to name but a few), this can sometimes be a challenging task. When you taste a great wine, though, you know the vineyard manager has succeeded, and when you taste a good wine, you know he hasn't made too bad a job of it.

There is, though, one very important exception to the 'healthy grapes' rule, and it's worth mentioning it here. One of the fungal colonisers of the vine is called *Botrytis cinerea*. Most occurrences of botrytis (more commonly known as grey rot) make the vineyard manager's heart sink: it can affect leaves, flowers and fruit, reducing the crop drastically; if rotten grapes are not separated out before vinification, it can make red wine look pale, and all wine taste bitter and mouldy. Botrytis flourishes in mild, damp conditions. Making sure the grapes grow in open, airy conditions is the best safeguard, but repeated chemical sprays are a more common (and ultimately less effective) weapon.

If you've ever tasted a rich, fatty, unctuous Sauternes, though, or a steamroller-like German Beerenauslese dessert wine, or a glass of complex, crisply defined sweet Tokaji, then you need to thank

the nimble-spored mushroom. Once certain varieties
of white grape are fully ripe, and under the right
weather conditions (a mixture, please God, of misty
mornings and bright, sunny, Indian-summer
afternoons), botrytis begins to marble golden grapes
with brown flecks, then turn them russet brown,
then shrivel them completely and cover them with
a grubby-looking beard. When they're tipped into
the press, a black cloud of spores explodes and
fills the cellar with storm clouds of decay. It looks
like a viticultural catastrophe of Chernobyl
proportions.

In fact what's happened is that the spores have
lanced their way into the grape and enjoyed an orgy
of water-drinking, acid-eating, sugar-nibbling,
glycerol-excreting, enzyme-producing, tannin-
liberating activity. In practical terms, the pressed
mouldy grapes produce a very sweet, complex juice,
whose fundamental balance and chemical
composition is quite different from what unaffected
grapes would yield. All the winemaker has to do is
coax this sticky, viscous stuff through a dawdling and
ultimately incomplete fermentation. The fungus has
made great sweet wine.

13
Grapes can be grown organically

Organic food is the future. Food, that is to say, which
has been grown without dousing the plant with
chemicals during its growing cycle, and without
poisoning the earth in which it spreads its roots –
earth in which the farmer hopes to grow crops again
next year, and which he hopes his son and grandson
will eventually cultivate after him. Everyone except
the chemist is in favour of organic food production.
Genetic engineering is a different matter (though

it's worth noting that genetic engineering could make organic agriculture much easier). So how's it going with organic vineyards and wine?

I had a holiday on a Greek island last year. The path to the nearest little beach wound its way through some pretty woods of baby cypress and pine. About half-way down, in a clearing, was what I thought at first was a sculpture garden. Only a closer look revealed that it was in fact a vineyard. A vineyard of blue vines. Now the moist, warm, salty air of an Ionian island is obviously not the ideal place for a vineyard, but these had been so heavily sprayed with copper sulphate solution that they appeared to be fashioned in verdigris, and I half-expected them to tinkle in the breeze. I've seen blue vines in Bordeaux and Italy, too, and in Champagne's precious vineyards I've seen shredded town rubbish dumped, as a kind of cheap fertiliser, complete with hundreds of thousands of scraps of the blue plastic bags issued by the municipality to collect the rubbish in the first place. Yes, since you ask; I am in favour of organic viticulture.

In one sense, though, it's not going very well. You don't see many 'organic wines' for sale – one or two, at best, on an off-licence shelf of several hundred lines. I don't, for example, have a single bottle in my cellar which proclaims itself on the label as 'organic'. (The French for organic wine, by the way, is *vin biologique*.)

A point to note is that much viticulture, by comparison with other forms of agriculture, is semi-organic anyway. Vines tend to grow in warm, dry, sunny places where disease problems are relatively uncommon; they don't like fertiliser; and high yields are undesirable because they have a negative effect on quality. That said, there are certain problems (like botrytis, described in the preceding section) which are very difficult to combat without some form of chemical intervention. Copper sulphate, the reason why those Greek vines were blue, is actually permitted for organic viticulture, albeit in greatly reduced amounts; so is sulphur.

Wine, furthermore, is not raw fruit, so even if you succeed in growing organic grapes you still have to practise organic winemaking if your wine is to qualify as 'organic'. This rules out many additions which winemakers (particularly in the New World) routinely use, such as ascorbic acid, employed as an anti-oxidant. Ascorbic acid, you might think, sounds sinister. Its other name is vitamin C.

So strict, by-the-rule-book organic wine production is in some ways a confused, questionable, perhaps even impossible ideal. The reality (and this is what French winegrowers call *la lutte raisonée*, 'the reasoned struggle') is that most serious wine-growers aim to be as organic as they can, respecting the purity of their fruit and their soils, but resorting to gentle remedies as and when they need to. I do worry about ingesting chemicals, but my concerns are chiefly with the food I eat and the polluted city air I breathe rather than the wine I drink.

This informal approach, of course, has no sanction to offer against lazy and incompetent winegrowers who use superfluous vineyard treatments and attempt to make up for deficiencies in their wine with heavy-handed chemical adjustments. I would certainly rather not drink the wine of a man who uses too much copper sulphate in the vineyard or has a winery full of old copper equipment, and then adds potassium ferrocyanide to get rid of excess copper in his wine. DDT, a suspected carcinogen, was once used routinely and enthusiastically in vineyards to combat insect pests; do we really know better today? Stricter labelling legislation, obliging winemakers to list residues and additives on back labels just as food manufacturers have to, is desirable; and organic viticulture remains the ideal. The difficult ideal.

14 Vines can be grown biodynamically

In addition to wines labelled as 'organic', you may also sometimes see wines described as 'biodynamic'. What's the difference?

Biodynamics is the agricultural branch of anthroposophy or 'spiritual science', a movement founded by Rudolf Steiner (1861–1925). In the words of Willy Schilthuis, author of *Biodynamic Agriculture*, "the biodynamic farmer works on the basis of an awareness or sense that every living being has a link with the spiritual cosmic world, and that it is the duty of every human ... to guide the life of these beings in such a way that these links can take place undisturbed. [Biodynamic farmers] work on the basis of the view that the Earth is a living organism and that a farm itself is a living organism." It is, if you like, organic farming with a strong, if hazy, spiritual charge.

Biodynamics is based on a series of agriculture lectures Steiner gave in present-day Poland the year before his death. With its unquestioned assumption of the reality of 'etheric and astral forces', its quaint preparations based on stuffing animal organs with flowers and then burying them ("in terms of its forces a deer bladder is almost a replica of the cosmos," is a typical Steiner aside), its primitive drawings and zany theorising, Steiner's book appears only intermittently sane. Yet his followers, most notably Ehrenfried Pfeiffer and Maria Thun, have adapted Steiner's ideas and turned them to a practical system of agriculture in which planetary, solar and lunar cycles determine the agricultural calendar, and in which Steinerist preparations in spray and compost form safeguard crop health and fertility. It would be of anecdotal interest only, were it not for the fact that a handful of France's greatest wine estates are now run, in whole or in part, along biodynamic lines: Leroy and Leflaive in Burgundy, Chapoutier in the Rhône valley, Huët in Vouvray and Coulée de Serrant in Savennières. These estates are so grand, in fact, that they don't always deign to mention biodynamics on the label. If, however, you see 'Demeter' mentioned on a label, this is the name which has been used for biodynamic products (including wine) in Germany and elsewhere since 1928. Intermittently: biodynamics and anthroposophy enjoyed the distinction of being banned by the Nazis.

Perhaps it is no accident that it is grand, rather than small-scale, estates which have succeeded with biodynamics. The fact that customers will pay a lot for your wine gives you the luxury of affording the risks inherent in radically organic viticulture. Leroy, for example, is a burgundy estate famous for two other things as well as biodynamics: its extraordinarily low yields in the vineyard, and its exceptionally high prices on merchants' lists. In general, however, biodynamically-produced wines from these estates are as good if not better than the non-biodynamically-produced wine of their peers.

Time will be the test. No matter how sceptical one might be about the means, it is hard not to disagree with the aim of biodynamics: its absolute belief in and respect for the plurality, sanctity and mystery of life itself. If it proves to be practically successful, for the producers of modestly priced wines as well as de-luxe ones, then ... the world will be a better place.

Part 2

The Winery: Making Wine

15 The winemaker as midwife

Before we poke our noses into the winery to find out what goes on there, let's briefly consider the role of the winemaker.

Wine is something which nature wants to happen. Juice seeps from ripe fruits; yeasts ride the air. When the two come into contact, as we'll see in section 19, fermentation occurs and wine is created. Wine, in this sense, predates human beings.

Where does this leave the winemaker? It's tempting to regard him or her in the same light as a painter in front of a bare canvas, or a chef standing in front of a box of ingredients with eight people expected for dinner in three hours' time. We relish the idea of the artist-hero, the craftsman-genius. Yet great European winemakers reject such comparisons firmly. "I'm just a midwife," said Noël Pinguet of Huët in the Loire valley's Vouvray region (a biodynamicist, by the way). "The less you interfere, the better wine is. I don't make wine; the wine makes itself. I'm just there to help with the transformation." Europeans believe that the style and character of a wine is created out in the vineyard, by its soil and its season; the winemaker's job is simply to ensure that nature expresses itself with maximum clarity in the glass. Indeed, French has no equivalent of the English word 'winemaker': it falls somewhere between *vigneron* (wine-grower, where the emphasis is on vineyard husbandry) and *oenologue* (oenologist – a technical consultant).

In Australia, New Zealand and California, by contrast, winemakers are regarded with more awe. You can see this in the notion of 'the flying winemaker', the technical guru who flies around the world with a head full of techniques and a bag stuffed with cultured yeasts, tartaric acid and oak chips – and then greatly improves the wine which the locals were previously botching. You can also see it in non-regional wines which are sold on the signature of the founder or winemaker, and which are all made to a certain style – such as Wolf Blass wines from Australia. Most big-selling branded wines are, in this sense, also winemaker's wines. Their bland, fault-free style tells you more about technology than a certain soil and a certain season.

To some extent, these differences have straight-forward causes. Australians, New Zealanders and Californians do not have a millennial tradition of wine-production to fall back on; they are also culturally pragmatic. Wine science developed to sophisticated levels in these countries because little was expected of vineyards. Researching great vineyard sites takes hundreds of years, so the way to make the best wine possible from an average vineyard site is to put as much effort as you can into winemaking.

More recently, both approaches have begun to be vindicated by 'the other side'. I haven't met a winemaker in the last half-decade who would disagree with the premise that 'great wine is made in the vineyard'. In every wine-growing country, more and more effort is going into growing the best fruit possible, and a heavy hand in the winery is less and less common. Wherever a winemaker believes he has a good or great vineyard to work with, his aim will be to give that vineyard a voice rather than shout his own style over the top of it.

At the same time, the shoddy winemaking which was once rife in much of Europe, even in its classic regions like Bordeaux and Burgundy, is now less and less common. The articulacy of great vineyards, Europeans have realised, does not emerge willy-nilly but can be strangled through poor winemaking; ordinary vineyards, by contrast, can be made to sing by a skilled winemaker. Even midwives, after all, need to practise impeccable hygiene, have a sound understanding of the principles of their work, and master the technical skills which will enable them to intervene when nature isn't taking the course it should.

16 All grape juice is white

Let's take a close look at a grape, first of all. It generally arrives at the winery as part of a bunch, attached to a stalk or stem (though mechanical harvesting actually shakes the berries off their stalks). Slice a grape in half, and you'll see that most of it is juice-bearing pulp; there's also skin, and there's pips. Generally speaking, the winemaker wants the skin and juice, but he doesn't want the stem and the pips. Exactly what he does next, though, depends on the kind of wine he wants to make.

Try crushing another grape from the same bunch between your fingers. Whatever the colour of the grape (and they vary from pale gold through vivid green to pink, red and black), you'll notice that the juice is white – or, to be more accurate, pale grey. This is the first important lesson of winemaking: all grape juice is white, even if the grapes are red. (There are some very rare exceptions to this rule, the most widely seen of which is a red-juiced variety called Alicante Bouschet.)

If all grape juice is white, where does the colour in red and rosé wines come from? The answer, of course, is the skins.

17 Red wine means maceration

OK: let's make some red wine.

There's a lorryload of red grapes outside. They

aren't, though, lying in the trailer in a big heap, bleeding juice all over the courtyard, but instead have been picked by hand into neat blue stackable boxes. Our exhausted, though surprisingly cheerful, winery workers empty the boxes of grapes into the steel reception bin, and the first thing we have to do is to get rid of the stems and crush the grapes. (If we wanted to make a particularly sturdy wine, we might leave some of the stems in with the grapes.)

All the colour in our red wine, as we now know, has to come from the grape skins, and so does its tannin (the dry, grippy textural element of red wines, similar to that found in strong black tea) and a number of its flavour compounds. We therefore have to leave the skins, together with the juice of the crushed grapes, to macerate. Exactly how we do this will define the exact style and depth of our wine.

There are lots of variables. For example, we might cool the juice and leave the skins to macerate before fermentation (if you want to know what fermentation is, turn to section 21); or we might ferment the wine with the skins straight away and leave the skins to soak in the wine for a week or two after fermentation has finished. The temperature of fermentation matters: cool ferments limit extraction and emphasise fruit flavours; warm ferments maximise extraction and produce earthy flavours. During fermentation, the skins and pips naturally float to the top of the vat or tank and form a thick, crusty 'cap' there. To increase extraction, this cap can be held under the surface of the wine with boards; we might also try spraying wine pumped out from underneath the cap over its surface. We could try punching it down with wooden batons; we might even take off all our clothes, jump in, and tread it down with our feet and legs. In Portugal, to make vintage port, the grapes are emptied into shallow granite tanks and the grape pickers spend their evenings marching up and down to music in a thick and pippy grape soup. It's important not to damage the pips, since they contain bitter oils which would spoil the wine. The human foot is just soft enough not to crush them. (I've done this, by the way, and it's hard work – the pips hurt. It also takes a week to get your toenails clean afterwards, but perhaps we won't go any further into this subject ...)

Once fermentation is over and we have extracted as much colour, texture and depth of flavour from the grape skins as we want, our raw red wine is made. What? Yes, of course you can try some.

Ah! You're spluttering. Violent, rasping, gassy and acidic? Well, perhaps I should have warned you. It will need a lot of finishing, it's true, but we'll pick up on that later. Let's get these skins and pips pressed first; we'll keep the press wine which remains, and if it's soft enough, and if we feel the wine needs a bit of beefing up, we might blend it back in later. We'll rot the leftovers down to make organic manure for the vineyard (or, occasionally, have them distilled to make a fiery spirit called marc in France or grappa in Italy).

As you can see, skins are all-important in red-wine making. I talked in 1997 to one of the leading château proprietors in Bordeaux's St Emilion region, the dapper Comte Stephan von Neipperg, and he said the aim of all of his fastidious 'garden work' in the vineyard was to grow red grapes with perfect skins. "I am a producer of skins," he said, beamingly smoothing the ends of his moustache into fine tips.

18 White wine means restraint

Red wine is a mess, and making it is the sort of process little boys would love to be involved with. Smashing, spilling, pulping, crushing, treading, staining: that's the point. You need to use the skins to stain and saturate and modify the pure white juice to the greatest possible extent. You don't worry overmuch about warmth in the air; you don't hurry.

White wine is the opposite: it's the product of restraint, delicacy, speed and coolness. White grapes are de-stemmed and crushed, just as our red grapes were, and the resulting grape soup is immediately drained and pressed, to separate the juice from the other components. Indeed the juice itself is divided up into free-run (the best) and pressed juice (not so fine, and sometimes discarded). Occasionally, the grapes, in uncrushed or crushed form, are refrigerated and stored for a few hours, giving the flavour elements in the skins a chance to infuse the juice. Generally, the juice is kept very cool and often protected scrupulously from air to stop it discolouring and tiring due to oxidation (though what always seems an implausible alternative to me is to hyper-oxidize the juice and let it recover later). The juice is clarified (by letting it stand and, sometimes, by centrifuging or filtering it) before fermentation – which is usually cool, thus slow.

And there you are: raw white wine. Want to try some? I think I will, too. Unlike red wine, it can taste delicious immediately after fermentation – very fresh and lively. Indeed in some countries, like Germany and Austria, the autumn's 'new wine' is sold when still half-fermented or only just finished, still milky with dissolved sediment and gas. It's served with warm, rich onion tart. You sit outside the winegrower's house to drink and eat, at picnic tables, as autumn turns mildly misty about you. Your glass will drive the dizzy little fruit flies wild with pleasure. They say the new wine and the onion tart 'make music' in the stomach. Excuse me ...

19
Rosé wine means compromise

Not a bad compromise, as anyone who's ever drunk a rosé for lunch in the South of France, within sight and earshot of the glittering, softly lapping Mediterranean, will confirm. You could also call it a white wine made with red grapes; sometimes, too, it's a by-product of serious red-wine making, particularly after a rain-spoiled harvest.

To make pink wine, you crush red grapes, then leave the juice in contact with the skins for a short while. Exactly how long depends on the grape type, but overnight is not untypical (hence the romantic-sounding *Vin d'une nuit* or 'wine of one night' description given to rosé from St Saturnin in the South of France). Press, and proceed as for white wine. If you want to make a very pale rosé (called blush or *vin gris*), you can press without any maceration; the pressure itself liberates a little colour. You can also blend red wine with white wine to make a rosé; this method is particularly popular for pink champagne.

To my taste, many of the best rosés are made by the 'by-product' method, called *saignée* in French (*saigner* means 'to bleed'). To do this, you 'bleed' juice off a harvest of crushed but as yet barely macerated red wine, then ferment the pink bleedings into a rosé wine. It improves the red wine, because there is then a smaller ratio of juice to skins (which is why it's useful after too much pre-harvest rain).

Why do I like these? Chiefly because they're made from better grapes than most rosé is. Pink wine's problem is that no one takes it very seriously, therefore no one plants grapes destined for pink wine in the best vineyard sites, using labour-intensive canopy management, old vines, low yields, and all the other stratagems for creating quality. If they did, there is no reason to suppose that pink wine couldn't be as good as any serious white. When a rosé results from the 'bleeding' of an ambitious red, it can thrill in its own right.

20 You don't have to crush

Just before we leave the first stage of winemaking, here's a few little footnotes.

You'll have noticed (if you were concentrating) that all our winemaking so far has involved crushing the grapes. For some wines, this is unnecessary: you begin with whole grapes on intact bunches.

If you press whole bunches, you're usually trying to make a very fine white wine. It's obligatory in Champagne, for example. Producers of red burgundy, too, often start off the maceration process with whole bunches of grapes.

You can also make very soft, perfumed and fruity red wines for drinking young by fermenting whole bunches of grapes in a sealed vat of carbon dioxide. Exactly what goes on here is rather complicated (its technical name is carbonic maceration); the most interesting aspect of it is that in its early stages alcohol is actually produced inside the grape without yeast, something most winemakers regard as akin to virgin birth. This is an enzymatic fermentation. Later on, normal fermentation takes over and finishes the process. If you've ever enjoyed bumpers of Beaujolais, either Nouveau or not, you'll be familiar with the bubblegum-scented, easy-drinking, lip-smacking style this method achieves.

21
Alcohol is a waste product

I've been wittering on about fermentation in the last few sections, but what exactly is it?

It's a chemical equation; it's an orgy; it's a miracle.

Chemically, fermentation means a glucose molecule being transformed into two ethanol molecules and two carbon dioxide molecules. The transforming is done by oxygen-starved yeasts; they do this in order to stay alive.

For 'glucose', read 'grape juice', and for 'ethanol', read 'alcohol'. Yeasts, in other words, eat the sugar in grape juice (and you only have to sip grape juice alongside apple juice to realise how much sugar it contains) and excrete alcohol and carbonic gas as waste products.

They carry on doing this until one of two things happens. Either they run out of sugar, leaving a dry wine; or the alcohol level rises to such an extent that (you could say) they drown in their own excrement: the alcohol kills them off. In the case of dessert wines, this should happen while there is still plenty of grape sugar left in the wine to give it a sweet taste.

Both the word 'yeast' and the word 'ferment' are derived from roots relating to boiling. This is the orgiastic side of the process: yeasts in warm sugar solutions multiply rapidly, and fermenting liquids appear to seethe and swarm. This is most spectacular not in wineries but in breweries, where the types of yeast used form spectacularly rocky heads on the fermenting beer tanks. If you want to slow the whole process down (as white-wine makers usually want to and as red-wine makers sometimes want to), you have to cool the vat. In cold, unheated cellars, an early winter can stop fermentation prematurely, accompanied by much cursing and swearing on the winemaker's part. He'll have to get the damn thing going again next spring.

And it's miraculous – or so it must have seemed to the winemakers of a thousand or two years ago. Since there are yeasts all around us, floating in the late summer air, fermentation will start of its own accord. The transformation the grape juice undergoes is startling – and the effects of alcohol on the human brain and body are profound. No wonder wine took on the symbolic force which it did, for example, in the Christian Eucharist.

Yeasts are all around us, and many winemakers, particularly in the classic European regions, are happy to rely on those: they know them and trust them. Winemakers in newer wine-producing countries tend to rely on cultured yeasts, since in these environments they give safer, more predictable results. If you can trust wild yeasts, they seem to produce more complex flavours; if you can't, of course, they may produce off-flavours, and are better avoided. (I was always told, by the way, that the bloom on grape skins contains yeast, but this is false. The bloom does, however, contain fermentation-soliciting yeast nutrients.)

A couple more things, before we leave fermentation. If you're making red wine and need to macerate grape skins, you'll have to use some sort of a vat, big or small, open or closed, at least until you've got the skin-bashing bit over and done with. If you're making white wine, by contrast, you can ferment in more or less any sort of a container – and, ladies and gentlemen, most significantly (and most expensively, and most troublesomely) in a barrel. A brand-new oak barrel. This, as it happens, is the subtlest way of giving a white wine oak flavours. If you want to know more immediately, turn to section 31.

Last of all: death. Carbon dioxide, that other by-product of this process, can kill winery workers.

It's invisible and odourless. It's also heavy, so it creeps over the edge of the vat and slides down on to the floor, where it collects like enmity. If it is not extracted, and the cellar isn't well ventilated, winery workers may not live to taste the fruit of their labours. Don't laugh: it has happened, many times.

22
Almost all reds and some whites ferment twice

Winter seems to be over. The morning light is brighter; the air is warm enough to linger in at midday. The mimosa tree by the winery door is a mass of livid yellow, while the blossom is swarming creamily in the almond trees. Winegrowers have, for hundreds of years, opened their cellar doors to let the new season in at this point. A little while after that, they would notice that the vats of red wine, vats which had finished their alcoholic fermentation in the gentle gloom and drizzle of November, begin 'working' again. If a candle is lowered towards the wine's surface, the flame gutters and expires: carbon dioxide is being produced. This they thought to be a second fermentation. The wine, growers knew, would taste better, easier, calmer once it was over.

What's happening, in fact, has nothing to do with yeasts, which by now are a sludge at the bottom of the vat. The agents for this transformation are lactic bacteria; they are converting malic acid in the wine into lactic acid and carbon dioxide. Malic acid is sharp and appley; lactic acid is soft and milky. The overall effect is to smooth out the stiff contours in new red wine. Almost all red wines, therefore, are put through 'malolactic', 'MLF' or 'malo', often immediately after alcoholic fermentation.

White wines, by contrast, sometimes benefit

from hanging on to their malic acid component: it gives them edge and definition, and broadens their spectrum of fruit flavours. For some white wines, therefore (such as German Riesling or wines made in the Loire valley from Sauvignon Blanc or Chenin Blanc grapes), the malo is avoided. Chardonnay, on the other hand, often tastes more appealing with a little milkiness or butteriness in place of those apple flavours, and from the structuring effect that the process seems to bring to the wine, so it is often put through malo in whole or in part. It all depends on local tradition (in Europe) or the effect the winemaker is aiming for (elsewhere). In Europe, malo generally happens naturally, provoked by populations of lactic bacteria in the winery air or in fermentation vessels; elsewhere a culture is added to the wine.

23
You can taste the summer

The wine's made, then: pure, natural, just as nature intended. We've been perfect midwives. Now let's put our feet up and treat ourselves to a little tasting.

Colour, first. What do you think? A bit darker than last year? Much darker? Or does it look like a light and elegant year to you?

Aroma, now. Powerfully fruity? Or just ... correct? Or is it not smelling of much, closed up, 'dumb'?

How about the flavours? Rich and concentrated, perhaps? Maybe a bit sharp? Or perhaps it's the opposite: fat, flaccid, lifeless. What about the tannins, the texture: is it tough and chewy? Or soft and silky? Does it lack concentration? Or is it dense, intense, tight and taut – ready for the cellar?

Wine is a book written by a season. Since the buds first began stirring, in the low sunshine of winter's end, the weather conditions of each minute of each day and each night have been physically registered and experienced by the vine, and that experience turned into fruit flavour. Vines are rooted in earth and stare at the sky. They can't go in and sit by the fire; they can't shelter from the wind, or unfurl umbrellas to keep the rain off. If the summer was cooler than usual, the wine might taste sharp. If the summer was very warm, the wine might taste rich and fat. If it rained a lot, particularly towards harvest, the wine might taste weak and dilute. These are the crude, broad outlines. What is remarkable about wine is its capacity for turning relatively subtle differences between seasons into flavours. No year is like another, and no vintage ever replicates the one which preceded it. When you taste a wine, you taste a summer.

Now let's rewind the film a little. If you're a winemaker, you will have followed the season and tasted the grapes. You'll have a fairly good idea (based on previous vintages) of roughly how your wine will turn out if you simply ferment it, no more and no less. That's why you may decide, before you even begin fermenting, to add something or other, to 'improve' on nature. Calculated subtly and intelligently, you may be right, and the wine may be better for your additions. Judge crudely and you may turn your wine into a grotesque. Let's see what happens.

24 You can add sugar or extra juice, or remove water

We're in Bordeaux, the year is 1992 and the date is October 7th. We have a problem. Over to you, Jacques.

"It all started pretty well: spring was early, flowering was perfect, the summer was hot. Then, towards the end of August, everything began to go wrong. On the last two days of August there were torrential rainstorms which tripled the normal monthly rain average – it was like a monsoon. The first part of September was dry, thank God, but very cool; ripening slowed right down. There was some more rain around the middle of the month, but we did have some good spells of clear weather between; we began harvesting the best parcels then. In October those terrible rains started all over again, and this time there was no end in sight. 'Just get the grapes in,' said the boss, so we did, but it was miserable: cold, soaking wet, mud everywhere. We had to leave half the grapes on the vines: they'd had it. What a mess."

In a year when everything goes perfectly, who wants to improve on nature? In a year when it doesn't, the eventual drinkers of the wine may be grateful for whatever the winemaker can do to improve matters.

Under such circumstances, there are two techniques a winemaker will generally use. The first, enrichment, is cheap; the second, concentration, very expensive.

Enrichment means adding sugar (from sugar beet; grape-derived syrups are also used) to the crushed grapes. This does not make the wine sweet, since the sugar will be fully fermented: it increases its final alcohol level, thus making it seem less 'thin', and bringing its acid levels (the winemaker hopes) into balance. It adds no fruit flavour, however. It doesn't make bad wine good; it just makes it less bad.

Concentration means getting excess water out of a wine without destroying its delicate flavour compounds, and there are two main ways of doing this. Under a vacuum, water evaporates at normal cellar temperatures: a machine called an evaporator will achieve this. Reserve osmosis is a technique for 'filtering' water out of wine based on its molecular size: another expensive machine. If you're broke, of course, you could just try a *saignée* (see section 19). Wine laws generally stipulate limits both for enrichment and concentration to keep the crassest malpractice in check.

Again, concentration doesn't save a bad vintage. Everything, remember, gets concentrated, including acid levels (which may already be unbalanced) and any off-flavours left by rotten grapes. If you're going to concentrate, you will have to separate out all the healthy grapes first.

Tough one, Jacques.

25 You can add or take away acid

"I'd love to grow good grapes. We're in the Iron Age of grape-growing right now. Things have gone to hell in a hat basket. We're always working with grapes that are good and not perfect. I'd love not to have to acidify." The speaker is Randall Grahm, California winegrower, Europhile, philosopher and ironist. He's not being ironic just now, though. He's sitting in London's Groucho Club answering questions from the sommeliers and wine merchants who buy his wines, and someone has just asked him whether he acidifies his wines or not.

At first glance, faced with nightmare harvests like that of Bordeaux in 1992, life seems a dream in the warm vineyards of countries such as Australia, Chile and California. The sun shines, mostly; the season ticks by; the grapes get riper and riper. The first autumn rains follow, mostly, at a respectful distance, waiting until fermentations are safely seething.

Yet behind every silver lining, as pessimists love to point out, is a cloud. You can't pick your grapes until they're ripe; and in such climates, full ripeness is often accompanied by relatively low acid levels. Low acid levels worry winemakers, especially those from technical rather than ancestral schools: not only do they fear their wines will taste flabby, but they also fear that they will turn brown easily, be unstable, and possibly be prey to yeast infections like brettanomyces. In the same way as winegrowers in cooler climates routinely enrich their musts, winegrowers in warm climates routinely add tartaric acid. Not only, indeed, do they add acid prior to fermentation, but also later, after malo, and even during blending. They claim that the effect is similar to enrichment for northern European wines – in other words, it brings balance to a wine. In truth, however, it is very different: acid is a much more prominent element of a wine's flavour than is the quiet, background presence of alcohol, and many acidified wines (particularly reds) are violently denatured and disfigured by this process.

Ambitious winemakers (like Randall Grahm) realise that great wine – wine which is not only memorable in flavour terms but which also expresses the uniqueness of a particular vineyard location – can only be made from grapes in which the proportions of sugar and acid have reached a natural equilibrium of their own, out in the vineyard. That is what is achieved in Europe's great winegrowing regions in good vintages, and that is what the more daring and successful winegrowers in hotter climates are working towards, too.

Before we leave acidity, a quick return to the horrors of the over-cold summer. Malolactic fermentation (see section 22) helps reduce over-high acidity but, if that still hasn't done the trick, deacidification is also possible (a parallel strategy to enrichment) by adding chalk to a wine. No one likes doing it; we're talking about making the best of a bad job here.

26
You can add chemicals or enzymes

This sounds alarming.

If you look at a complete list of permitted additives for wine, you may well become even more alarmed: it's long. Then you check the listed packet ingredients for the pre-cooked, frozen meal you're eating tonight because you haven't got time to cook, and for the ready-made, fluffy yellow dessert which follows it, and then for the toothpaste with which you're going to brush your teeth afterwards, and it will all alarm you so much that you won't be able to sleep, and you'll probably have to take a sleeping pill and we won't even talk about what goes into that. How is it we're still alive at all?

In fact, in contrast to the additions in preserved and ready-cooked foods, most of those permitted in wine are there for problem-solving purposes and are seldom used. Wine is, compared with cheese or meat products, intrinsically safe and stable. That was why, historically, it could be shipped away from the vineyard where it was produced and drunk by men in wigs in Stockholm or Savannah. The main substances which get added to wine are given below. We already know (from previous sections) about yeasts, lactic bacteria, sugar and acids; tannins are sometimes added to red wines, too.

1. Sulphur dioxide. We'll start with this, because almost no wine is ever made without it (it is, indeed, a natural by-product of fermentation). It's used to disinfect equipment and bottles, to prevent fresh grapes from oxidising, to kill bacteria and wild yeast, to promote a swift fermentation, to improve colour, to aid extraction during maceration, and to prevent sweet wines from re-fermenting. Used discreetly, you won't notice it. Used carelessly, you'll notice it either catching in your throat and burning your nose in young wines (free sulphur), or forming

stinky, pongy, eggy aromas in older ones (hydrogen sulphide and mercaptans). More on this in section 45.

2. Enzymes. A range of these may be added to help along such winemaking processes as the settling of freshly pressed juice before white-wine fermentation, the extraction of flavour compounds from certain varieties, and fermentation itself.

3. Finings. These are materials added to wine to help its clarification. The most traditional additive, still widely used throughout Europe, is egg white; others include isinglass (from fish swim bladders), bentonite (a clay), casein (from milk) and gelatine. Little or no trace of these remains in the finished wine, though they may strip flavour out of a wine along with the impurities they are removing.

27
You can add extra alcohol

Everything we've added to our wine in the last three sections has been aimed at remedying the deficiencies of nature, or smoothing the winemaking process on its way. We're going to add something now which will make a different type of wine altogether.

It's alcohol – usually in the form of very strong grape brandy. You'll remember from section 21 that yeasts finish their work and die when one of two things happen: either they run out of sugar, or the alcohol polishes them off. The possibilities presented by this are interesting. What if, say, you began fermenting a wine and then added extra alcohol to it half-way through its fermentation, thereby knocking the yeasts out of it? It would still have some of the delicious 'wininess' which fermentation gives, but it would also remain sweet, since around half its natural grape sugars would remain unfermented. Could be delicious, don't you think?

And you're right: it's called port. Adding alcohol to a wine is known as fortification. There are a number of different ways of doing this.

You can, for example, skip the fermentation bit altogether, and just add alcohol to grape juice. The technical name for this is a 'mistelle': it's how Pineau des Charentes is made (Cognac plus grape juice) and Floc de Gascogne (Armagnac plus grape juice) and even Normandy's Pommeau (Calvados plus apple juice). Anything French called a *vin de liqueur* is made in this way, as are some Spanish Moscatel wines.

Fermentation produces flavours of its own which help add complexity, so the greatest fortified wines are all made by adding alcohol half-way through fermentation (port, Bual or Malmsey Madeira, French *vins doux naturels*, Australian Liqueur Muscats and Tokays) or even after fermentation has finished (sherry, Verdelho and Sercial Madeira). Alcohol is a great preservative, so all of these wines are relatively stable and robust. Historically, indeed, they generally came into being in order to cope with long sea journeys and still taste good at the other end. This robustness presents other possibilities – as we'll discover in section 29.

28 You can trap bubbles in bottles

Remember the killer vat we encountered a few sections ago? While the yeasts are busy turning sugar into mirthful alcohol, saturnine CO_2 is lumbering up off the fermenting wine, sliding over the vat edge and tumbling, like an obese and malicious ghost, down on to the floor.

Now let's use a little imagination to turn this gas to some use. If you sealed up the vat at the beginning of fermentation, it would probably explode. Disaster! If you sealed it up towards the end of fermentation, it would contain dissolved gas. And what does dissolved gas do in a wine? Why, it makes it sparkle, froth and fizz. Fun!

This, in principle, is how you get the bubbles into sparkling wine. There are, of course, lots of variants on the technique. The most entertainingly primitive I have ever come across is something called *chèvre* (goat) in Savoie and Switzerland: grape juice set to ferment in small, reinforced, sealed barrels which look as if they could be used to transport spent nuclear fuel. Eventually the yeasts are killed not by alcohol but by gas pressure. Open the tap, and out shoots a glassful of sweet froth.

If you simply finish fermentation in sealed containers (such as corked bottles), you will produce a crude sparkling wine with a sediment in it. Wines are produced in this way in France's Gaillac (where it is called the *méthode ancestrale* or *rurale*) and, with an intervening filtration, for Clairette de Die Tradition.

The vast majority of sparkling wines, though, are produced by adding yeast and sugar to a 'base' wine which has already finished fermentation. This re-starts the whole process; it can be effected in a tank or in a bottle. It produces a little more sediment, of course, since the dead yeast has to fall somewhere, and a few wines are sold with this sediment still in the bottles; traditional, authentic Lambrusco is one of these. (Beer-drinkers are much more familiar with this than wine-drinkers: all 'bottle-conditioned' beers are sold with their sediment, and most wheat beers are, too.)

If you don't want the sediment clouding and flavouring your wine, there are various nifty ways for removing it. Filtration under pressure would be one – this is used for wine which acquires its sparkle in tanks (this is called *cuve close* in French or the

Charmat process elsewhere), and for wines transferred from one bottle to another (*transvasement* in French; this 'transfer method' is also much used for inexpensive Australian sparkling wines, which will say 'bottle fermented' on the label).

The very best sparkling wines and Champagnes, though, are always made by a slow, second fermentation in a bottle, followed by an ageing period (the longer the better); the dead yeast is still sealed up with the wine, imparting some of its 'biscuity' flavours to it. Eventually, the bottles are turned upside-down, meaning that the dead yeast edges gradually down into the neck. The neck is then frozen, the bottles turned the right way up again, the plug of yeast is ejected by the pressure of the gas in the bottle, and the bottles are topped up with sweet wine and corked again, before the gas has a chance to escape. This was once called the *méthode champenoise* and is now generally known as 'the traditional method'; Australian sparkling wines made in this way will say 'Fermented in this bottle'.

Oh, and there's one other way of making sparkling wine, too. Just pump gas into it, as you would to make a fizzy drink. Subtle? No; but it can be fun, too.

29
Wines need air

Wines need air just as humans need minerals. A little is essential; a lot is fatal.

It varies, of course: we'll come to the exceptions at the end of this section. In the main, though, wines need to be protected from air (or, more accurately, from oxygen) to stop them either becoming flat, brown, dull and tired (at which point they are called 'oxidised') or vinegary. Physical protection is ideal: this means storage in neutral containers filled full at all times, or beneath blankets of inert gas such as nitrogen. Sulphur provides an element of chemical protection, as does ascorbic acid. Keeping wine cool, and moving it around as little and as gently as possible, will also help keep enemy oxygen at bay. Putting it in a sealed bottle, finally, is an anti-oxidative measure.

And yet ... have you ever opened a bottle of wine and found it stinky? And then discovered, to your astonishment, that the problem disappears by the end of the bottle? If so, that's proof that wines need a little oxygen from time to time.

The shadow process of oxidation is called reduction, and wines in an over-reduced state expose their sulphur compounds to drinkers like strange men in raincoats exposing their genitals to pretty girls. The solution is to shame the wine into politer behaviour with the publicity of oxygen – by decanting it a couple of times, for example.

In the cellar, wines need air to get fermentation going, and to help the ageing process along. The latter – transferring wine from one barrel to another – is called 'racking'. It has other benefits, too, like lifting a developing wine off the sediment it has produced. This kind of positive oxidation is known as aeration, and judging it correctly is a key wine-making skill. And wine-drinking skill, too: turn to section 97 for more details.

The exceptions affect, in the main, fortified wines – for the simple reason that, once you get above 15 per cent alcohol, exposing a wine to oxygen no longer carries the same risk of ending up as vinegar. Exposing fortified wines to oxygen can create very interesting, nutty flavours (and, through evaporation, great concentration of flavour, too). Tawny port is mildly oxidised; oloroso sherry is oxidised to a major extent; and Vintage Madeira is massively, majestically oxidised – so much so, indeed, that you can keep a bottle open for three or four months with no appreciable loss of quality. Indeed, with Madeira, we extend the concept of oxidation into something called 'maderisation', which means exposure not only to oxygen but also to heat. See section 79 for more.

Any wine stored in a barrel, though, will be oxidising very gently, so a little oxidation is an important flavour creator for all of the greatest red wines, and some of the greatest whites, too. There are some regions, moreover, like the Jura in France, where pronounced oxidation is a regional style. Some oxidation, too, takes place through the cork, while a wine is in bottle: a little if it's lying down; rather more if it's standing up (and the cork is thus shrinking). That's one reason why you should keep your bottles lying down if you want to drink them more than a month or so after you bought them.

30 Not all wines are oaked...

Wine is a child of time as well as place. A glass of milk, one hopes, was a green gleam in a cow's placid eye just a week or two earlier; a glass of wine, by contrast, is usually at least two seasons old and, not unusually, two or more years old. It needs time to soften and round out, to calm itself, to settle into stability, to ease into harmony. In what?

The most famous and flavorous container for wine after (and sometimes during) fermentation and before bottling is a small oak barrel: more of this in the next section. The sort of oak storage which imparts flavour is not essential, though: you can also store wine in old barrels or larger tuns of old oak, in stainless-steel vats and tanks, and in vats and tanks made of other materials (such as fibreglass). All of these containers are, or should be, 'neutral': they leave the flavour of the wine unchanged. The only difference between them is that large tuns of old oak will allow the wine to breathe and soften a little, whereas filled stainless-steel vats will keep it brightly protected from air.

In the ferment of winemaking aspiration which marked the last two decades of the twentieth century, oak became identified with 'the taste of quality' in many emerging wine cultures for most Chardonnay-based white wines and most red wines. Storing wine (or, as the French say, 'bringing wine up': *élevage*) in neutral containers offers other possibilities, in particular the creation of fruit aromas and flavours of great character and purity. It's likely that we will see many more wines from Australia, Chile, South Africa and California in the twenty-first century that are 'unoaked' and proud of it. Some great grape varieties (most notably Riesling) are nearly always unhappy when their flavours are muddied by oak; and those wine regions whose speciality is aromatic white wines (such as Alsace and Germany) have little use for small oak barrels.

31 ..but wine likes oak

Let's take a walk in the forest. Since it's imaginary, why don't we set off for our walk at dawn? On a summer's day, say, when the first sunlight comes ruffling warmly through the low, dewy grasses, and the space between the trees seems charged with the misty, moist blue of absence itself.

This forest, as you see, is carefully managed: there's no tangle of scrub underfoot, no storm-felled relics gently decomposing in a festival of lichen, ivy and bracket fungus. Instead, sentry-like oaks soar skywards, their lower branches neatly pared away leaving little flurries of twig to commemorate the wound, their trunks as evenly textured as water below a quiet mill race.

These trees, reaching maturity as a crop, would be a century-and-a-half old, planted at around the same moment that Dickens was putting the final full stop at the end of *David Copperfield*. Treat yourself to a top Californian Chardonnay today, and the oak you'll taste in the wine, lending it the riches of butter and spice and the texture of heavy silk, might have been planted as Dickens first nibbled his pencil before beginning *The Pickwick Papers*.

Oak barrels were initially used to store wine, by the Romans, as a convenience. Other woods could be used (chestnut has its followers, even today), but oak is unmatched for malleability and impermeability; unlike earthenware amphorae, oak casks are robust, and can take a knock or two without surrendering their contents to earth or ocean. Nowadays, as we saw in the last section, there are many alternatives for storing your wine, almost all of them, moreover, vastly cheaper than oak. So why persist?

Flavour, in a word. The flavour of 150-year-old oak wood seems to be the perfect complement to fine fermented grape juice; the two plants seem made for one another. Oak can, of course, be overdone. "Those who consider oak a primary flavour for wine are akin to those who consider ketchup as a vegetable," says California winegrower Randall Grahm. But subtly layered into a wine, it adds enormous pleasure and complexity. New oak will play a role in at least 80 per cent of the world's finest wines.

Three varieties of oak are chiefly used. The first is the brown oak (also known as the sessile or durmast oak: *Quercus sessiliflora* or *Quercus petraea*); when you see 'French oak' referred to on back labels, this is generally what is meant. It's a slow-growing forest oak which likes poor, sandy soils, and yields a tight-grained wood with many aromatic compounds.

The second type is the white oak (*Quercus alba*), referred to as 'American oak' on labels. This is faster growing, and its cell structure means it can be sawn rather than split as French oak must be; this in turn means that more of the tree is usable (50 per cent rather than 15 per cent), so American oak barrels are much cheaper than French. It provides different flavours, too. All oak gives wine a sweet taste since, when lignin is broken down by heat, it produces syringaldehyde and vanillin; indeed most of the vanilla essence used in bakery products comes not from vanilla pods but from wood. Yet American oak produces much more intensely vanillic and coconut-like flavours than does the more discreet French oak. It suits some wines – Australian Shiraz-based reds, for example, or reds made from Tempranillo in Spain's Rioja region – more than others.

There is, finally, a third type of oak: the fast-growing, coarse-grained, broad-crowned pedunculate oak (*Quercus robur*), which is also used for wines, though its plentiful tannins tend to give them a harsh and woody character. It would generally be referred to on labels as Limousin oak, since this region is where France's main supply of pedunculate oak comes from. Its tannic profusion makes it ideal for ageing spirits such as Cognac, for which it is the oak of choice.

Oak trees hybridise easily, so the clarity of these distinctions is not always evident to coopers purchasing wood. You may also see specific forest or French *département* names mentioned on labels (Tronçais is an example of a forest; Allier of a *département*).

Oak must be seasoned and dried before it is used, and this is another important factor in the quality equation (slow air-drying is infinitely preferable to fast kiln-drying). So important, indeed, that at least one fine-wine wine producer, Angelo Gaja of Piedmont in Italy, insists on buying and ageing all his own oak before having it coopered. Fire is used to shape and finish oak casks, and this leaves a char or 'toast' on their interior surfaces. A light toast of 30 minutes or so accentuates spicy characters; a fuller, 40-minute toast emphasises vanilla and butter; 50 minutes would constitute a heavy toast, giving wine smoky and, literally, toasty flavours.

The standard size for a small oak cask is the *barrique* (around 225 litres). Other sizes you might see mentioned include hogsheads (315 litres), puncheons (450 litres), pipes (a shipping pipe is 534 litres, but pipes in port lodges are 580 to 630 litres) and butts (600–650 litres). High-quality white wines are generally individually fermented in new-oak casks; this is called barrel-fermentation, and gives much subtler, softer, creamier oak flavours than fermenting wines in stainless-steel vats and then running them into oak casks for ageing (which makes them taste 'woody'). Red wines tend not to be fermented in oak casks because of the need for effective maceration: it's hard to get all those skins and pips in and out of a barrel. Sometimes (especially in Australia), red wines are pressed and poured into barrels to finish their fermentation there; and it is becoming standard practice for fine red wines to go into cask as soon as possible, when they are still warm, before they have undergone their malolactic fermentation.

The proportion of new oak used for fermenting and ageing wines varies greatly. Around 50 per cent new oak has traditionally been standard for serious Bordeaux reds, for example, but recently it has become fashionable among the ambitious to give their wines '150 per cent' or '200 per cent' new wood. What the heck does '200 per cent new wood' mean? It means that not only does all the wine go straight into new wood, but that it goes once again into new wood at the moment of its first racking. Vegetables or ketchup? The drinker must decide.

Such strategies, evidently, cost a lot. There are much cheaper alternatives: you can dunk staves into your wine as it merrily ferments in a stainless-steel vat, or shake a bag of oak chips into it. It will taste 'oaked'. You can't make great wine like that, but you can make surprisingly good wine using staves and chips – known, tongue-in-cheek, as *Quercus fragmentus*.

32
Easy does it: the winemaker's farewell

So there it is, your beautiful wine. You nursed the grapes through a season to ripeness and laboriously harvested them by hand; you spent a few sleepless nights during an anxious month as you oversaw maceration and fermentation; since then the wine has been through its malolactic fermentation and has been gently calming itself for a year or so in frighteningly expensive oak casks. You taste it from time to time, using the glass syphoning tube called a wine thief – and it tastes excitingly delicious. All that effort was worthwhile. You just need to get it into bottle, then you're done. Don't blow it now, eh?

Funnily enough, it is precisely at this moment that many excellent red (and, to a lesser extent, white) wines are spoiled. And we're all to blame.

We're to blame, because somehow or other we have grown to expect wines won't have 'bits' in. If we see bits, gunge, sediment, we may think something has gone wrong with the wine. It may look and taste fine, but we still take it back and ask for something else, or want our money back. We confuse purity and sterility.

We all want pure wine – pure living wine. We want little wines capable of communicating their personalities forcefully; we want grand wines capable of blossoming and growing more articulate in the bottle as the years pass. We don't want sterile wine – technically correct but pallid, lifeless, with all the personality and exuberance stripped out of it, incapable of acquiring anything with the years save a tired frown.

All wine should be bottled and sold in a stable state. Stability means that the wine will not referment in bottle, or undergo bacteriological degradation; either would make it smell and taste either strange or repellent. It doesn't, though, preclude sediment. You could call sediment wine's laughter lines. It is, in other words, a natural, healthy and welcome side-effect of ageing. Red wines and fine ports are most prone to throw sediments, sometimes heavy ones; but it is perfectly natural for white wines to produce sediments, too, especially of tartrate crystals (which worried consumers sometimes mistake for glass fragments).

If you let a wine take its time, in most cases it will achieve this stability naturally. After fermentation, it will deposit a heavy sediment; as it matures in tank or cask, it will continue to deposit lighter sediments. Eventually it 'falls bright', becoming clear and stable. You could bottle it then, and it would probably be fine.

Alas, 'probably' isn't good enough for the modern world. Wine producers in Burgundy or the Barossa need the certainty that when their wines are placed on the table next to a bleeding 12-oz steak in a fancy restaurant in downtown Amarillo, with the digital neon thermometer on the local radio building across the street reading 33°C under a waxing moon, the drinkers are going to have themselves a real good time. You can't fool with stability. Stability is security; security is profit.

So it all gets overdone, and wines which should have been pure and expressive end up sterile and mute.

There are three chief techniques for stabilising wines. The first is cold-stabilisation: chilling and holding wine at a temperature of around −3°C (27°F) for a day or two, in order to precipitate out its tartrate crystals.

The second is called fining: it means adding a coagulating agent which sinks through the wine, collecting soluble substances or proteins in the wines which may form hazes or precipitate later. Egg whites, isinglass (from fish swim bladders), gelatine and a superfine clay called bentonite are all used for this purpose.

The third technique is filtration: passing wine through a physical barrier to remove particles in it. It can be done immediately after fermentation, during racking procedures and (most commonly of all) before bottling.

Wines are also (though rarely) centrifuged and even pasteurised in order to ensure stability.

Don't misunderstand me: for many young wines, especially those which contain sugars, sterility is essential. White Lambrusco, for example, would not be possible without sterile filtration. Since it's going to be drunk within a matter of weeks in any case, the issue of bottle evolution is immaterial.

For the vast middle-ground of wines, however, and for all fine wines, fining and filtration needs to be undertaken with extreme care, if at all. It's yet another way in which one winemaker can prove his or her mastery over another. Not necessarily by saying 'I never fine or filter' (though bottling stable wines that have been neither fined nor filtered is an achievable ideal); but above all by knowing the very minimum intervention required in order to release a lovingly crafted wine into the world with its personality and its future intact.

Part 3

The Cellar: Ageing Wine

33 Cool, dark and damp: wine's dream home

Come with me on a flying visit to Hungary.

Let's leave the car here, and take this little winding path up through the vineyards. We're in the north-east of the country, in the Tokaji region – a land of quiescent volcanoes now green with vines and topped with forest. See that door up there, behind the iron grill, set into the hillside? Here's the keys, on this old iron hoop. Let yourself in. There's candles and matches on the right-hand side as you go in. You'll be amazed at what you see, I promise. I'll wait for you here. I want to sit in the sunshine.

[Pause. Time passes. Birds fly by. Vines bask in light. Unseen physiological processes occur. Footsteps return down the stony path.]

Told you. Yes, it must go about a quarter of a mile into the hill, easily. Aren't those drapes and swags of puffy mould extraordinary? I always think the bottles, with that mould swarming all over their necks, look like guardsmen wearing bearskin hats. It's damp, sure; darker than night. No, the temperature never varies: you'd be surprised how warm that 11°C feels in the winter, when there's snow blowing around the vineyards and you walk in there with your winter coat buttoned tight; but just now, in the middle of August, in jeans and a teeshirt, it feels soothingly cool.

Thus Tokaji wine grows ancient. Almost all wines (Madeira would be the only conceivable exception) relish the same kind of conditions in order to age perfectly: darkness, dampness, a steadily cool temperature. In such conditions, wine ages as slowly as it can, breathing almost imperceptibly through the medium of a moisture-charged cork. If it's stored in warmer, lighter, dryer conditions, it will age more quickly and perhaps less successfully.

What happens to wine as it ages? Red wines lighten in colour, and change hue – from purple-black to red-brown. Their aromas and flavours evolve, too. Simple wines thin out and lose definition and interest. Complex wines not only acquire a measure of harmony which might have been missing in youth, but often become more articulate, with a seductive range of aromas, softened tannins, and flavours in which the fruits of youth have been replaced by a much broader spectrum of savoury or earthy flavours. Technically speaking, much of this is due to the polymerisation of phenolics. (Phenolics are reactive chemical compounds based on phenol: wine phenolics include colour pigments, tannins and some flavour compounds. Polymerisation is the process by which simple phenolic molecules combine to form larger, more complex molecules. Sediment in the bottom of the bottle is the physical result of this process.)

White wines generally deepen in colour as they age, eventually acquiring a brown hue. Harmony and articulacy of scent and flavour are the goals of white-wine ageing as much as red, though a lower proportion of white wines has any ageing potential. Dessert white wines based on grapes affected by noble rot (see section 12) tend to age well, becoming slightly dryer as they do so. Some fortified wines, like vintage port and Madeira, are destined to age well over a very long period, whereas others (like fino sherry) need to be drunk as soon as possible after bottling. We'll examine cellaring strategies in more detail in the next section.

If you're lucky enough to have a real cellar at home, make the most of it. Don't even worry if it's not as cool as our Hungarian hillside; as long as the temperature is relatively steady from day to day, not varying by more than half a degree or so overnight (and by seven or eight degrees in total between winter and summer), you'll get good results. Make sure the wines are lying on their sides: this keeps their corks moist, which in turn stops excess oxygen getting into the bottles or wine getting out. Wines hate physical movement, so take care not to place them next to any vibrating machinery.

If, like me, you don't have a cellar in your house, improvisation is necessary. Look for naturally cool, still, dark, dampish corners of the house for your wine racks. I have some in an understairs cupboard, which is ideal for darkness and stillness but not as cool as I'd like and rather too dry; so I also have some in the laundry-room, which is cool and dampish though light. Old sheets and blankets, draped over the racks, keep these bottles in the dark. If I had a reasonably well-insulated garage (which I don't), I might be tempted to keep some more wine there. Kitchens and attics are to be avoided. Improvised storage of this sort is fine for drinking stocks over a year or two, but I keep anything seriously good which needs storing for years with professional wine-storage companies: you'll find the names and addresses of these advertised in wine magazines.

34
It's ready when it tastes good

Exhibit A: a dead mackerel. Exhibit B: an apple. Exhibit C: a bottle of wine.

One look at Exhibit A tells you to leave it well alone. Its beautiful silver and blue iridescence has gone; its taut skin is slackening; its eye is bloodshot and dull; it stinks.

Exhibit B is slightly more difficult. At first glance it looks enticing, but once you give it a little yielding squeeze you realise that it won't be great eating. It hasn't yet got to the wrinkly shrivelled stage, though, and there's no brown and pulpy bruises; it will pass.

And Exhibit C? This is a tricky one. It looks perfect from the outside, but the label tells you it's ten years old. Should it have been drunk nine years ago, or is it just coming into its own? Has it been sitting on top of a radiator and next to a heavily used tumble dryer for the last nine years, or has it been slumbering dreamlessly in a deep, dark cellar? The only way you can tell is by pulling the cork and getting in there – which, if you've only got one bottle, is too late. There's no putting the cork back afterwards. To enjoy wine, you must destroy it.

Immature red wines tend to taste rather hard and violent, since their tannins and flavour components haven't yet settled down and acquired harmony; immature white wines, by contrast, tend to taste duller than you expect, since only time will bring them articulacy. Over-aged red wines taste thin, sour and weedy; over-aged whites can taste like that, too, but they can also taste fat and flat.

Don't get too anxious, though; these extreme situations don't occur often. Around 90 per cent of all wines are ready to drink when you buy them, and this includes all inexpensive wines. Back-of-bottle labels sometimes optimistically proclaim that a particular wine 'can be drunk now, but will improve with up to three years' further cellaring'; in most cases, this is misleading. I have experimented extensively with storing all sorts of wines for periods of up to 10 years and, in general it is only the classic wines of Europe (most notably the best from Bordeaux, Burgundy, the Rhône and Loire valleys, Piedmont, Tuscany and Germany, plus the best port and Madeira) that truly improve with cellaring. Many other wines, especially broad-shouldered New World reds, hold their qualities very well over surprisingly long periods of a decade or more – but what's the point of storing something unless it will incontrovertibly improve?

Even lesser wines from these classic areas have relatively short ageing trajectories. Mid-priced claret and burgundy, for example, is probably going to be at its best at around five to seven years after the vintage, and I personally consider vintage port at its best at between ten and 18 years old, rather than the 30 or so years sanctified by British tradition. There is ample evidence that those bitten by the wine bug frequently store wines too long; indeed there is a general misunderstanding among consumers that all wine improves with storage. Some of my saddest professional moments have been invitations to inspect lovingly assembled and treasured collections of wine never intended for keeping for longer than a few months. Ten years on, their proud owners assume that time's alchemy will have gilded them. In fact, all the pleasure tiptoed away years ago, leaving behind the shrunken lineaments of what the wines once were. The owners invited me to a baptism. I have to tell them it's a funeral.

To sum up, then: drink most wine as soon as you buy it. If you're going to buy immature fine wines from Europe's classic areas, make sure you have somewhere suitable to store them, and try to buy at least three bottles at a time. The retailers selling you these expensive bottles will generally offer advice about when to drink them. Try one of the three bottles at the earliest counselled opportunity, and see what it's like. Does it taste good to you? If so, it's ready. Get stuck in, and don't worry about it. As a traditional port man once said to me (mixing his metaphors alarmingly), "Infanticide is better than necrophilia".

35
Cork is oak bark

We pressed on into the heart of the forest, the car
bumping its way down the pitted rides. Eventually
we reached a clearing containing what looked at first
glance like three or four small wooden huts. Closer
inspection revealed them to be large ricks of tree
bark. Two men were emptying drainpipe-shaped
pieces of bark from a trailer and stacking them,
chatting as they did so in lazy-vowelled Portuguese.
"You want to see the pickers?" asked the driver of
the huge, high-axled tractor. "Climb on board."

And so off we lurched into the open forest
scrub, the tractor taking every obstacle in its stride.
Twice the driver stopped, turned off the engine and
listened for voices in the still, warm afternoon air.
Then we'd press on.

Finally, we found them, the cork-pickers:
nimble, axe-wielding men shouldering small
aluminium ladders with which they'd swiftly
scramble up to the cleft in the squat cork oaks.
One hack, two; then they'd lever off, with the axe's
tapered haft, a long segment of cork bark. Their
wives, wearing straw hats and pinnies, would stack
and sort the bark behind them. They kept water cool
in earthenware pitchers, which the men would lift,
with the crook of their arms, to drink from when
they needed refreshment.

Cork is the bark of a tough little evergreen oak
tree: *Quercus suber*. The tree trunks, denuded,
glowed smooth and rose-red in the dappled sunlight.
It was a shocking sight, somehow, like seeing a rabbit
skinned alive. Why don't the trees die? The answer
is that the phloem (the nutritive transporting tissue)
in cork oaks is sited underneath an internal growth
layer (the cambium), rather than between the
cambium and the bark, as in most trees. Even so, the
stripping is a vulnerable moment for the tree, which

is why it takes place between June and August, when vegetative growth is at a maximum. By leaf-fall, the rose-red has faded to grey; bark begins to reappear the following year.

The trees are left alone for the first thirty years of their lives before being 'unmasked' or stripped for the first time. From then on, stripping takes place every nine years. Once harvested, the bark is stored to season for six months or so, then baled and boiled in giant pits of hot water. A 'ripening' period of a few weeks follows, then the bark is cut, classified and punched into corks before being printed, dried and finished with silicon and other coatings. Portugal is, by some way, the world's leading supplier of cork, most of which is grown in the sandy, potassium-rich soils of the Alentejo and the Algarve; Spain and North Africa have extensive forests, too.

Look at a cork through a microscope and you'll see a snowscape of the finest sponge. This is composed of millions of 14-sided cells (600 million in the average cork), each of which is filled with a nitrogen-oxygen mixture locked into the cells by a waxy substance called suberin. This structure gives cork its remarkable pliability and impermeability. The structure is broken by crevasse-like lenticels from time to time – pores which permit gas exchanges between the inside of the tree and the exterior. High-quality corks are long, smooth, and have few lenticels; low-quality corks are short and may have many lenticels. The cheapest corks of all are compounded from cork agglomerate or dust.

Cork has been used to stop wine vessels since Greek times, and is ideal for the purpose, since the very slow exchanges a moist cork permits with the air are ideal for allowing wines to mature gradually.

They do, however, have one serious flaw. Read on.

36
Corkiness is a taint, not a foreign body

What follows is true in every detail.

I finished writing section 35 yesterday afternoon, went off for a swim in the local municipal pool, then came home and set about tasting nine wines (which I was researching for a newspaper article) before cooking dinner. The tasting was due to end with the Grand Red, the top-of-the-range £14 masterpiece. One sniff, and I groaned inwardly. It didn't smell of earth, undergrowth and herbs as I hoped. It smelled sweetly musty, of fetid mushrooms and damp cardboard, of chemical decay. It was corked.

I needed to make some sort of sense of this wine, so I pressed on, ferreting about for 'real' aromas and flavours, for perceptible tannins and some notion of fruit and acid balance, beneath this vaguely nauseating blanket. It was difficult, and profoundly unsatisfactory; corkiness is impossible to ignore. Not only does it, like schizophrenia in humans, rob a wine of its true personality, but it is also hugely monotonous. Wines can be slightly corked or extensively corked; once present, the taint does not disappear. (Bits of cork ejected by the corkscrew and floating in the wine, by the way, do not a 'corked' wine make. They are just ... bits of cork. Fish 'em out with a spoon.)

This was a sample which had been sent to me, though I have several cases of a different vintage of the same wine in my cellar. At £13.35 a bottle. Galling: a corked wine means your money has been wasted, your moment of pleasure lost.

The compound to blame is called 2,4,6-trichloroanisole, known as TCA for short, and is detectable at extraordinarily low concentrations of a few parts per trillion. The chlorine bleaching of corks is thought to be responsible, and the offending cork, sure enough, had been bleached; other methods are now being employed by cork processors for the same disinfectant end. For inexpensive wines, though, it may be too late: alternative closures are on the rise. There may be lean times ahead for the cork industry, for those nimble pickers I saw, for that beautifully open, light-strewn forest in southern Portugal.

37
'Corks' can be plastic, too

Unless you're wealthy enough to drink nothing but expensive wine, you'll already be familiar with them. Rock-star purple, sunshine yellow, widow black, the plastic cork could be said to have brought a little more fun to wine drinking. They're made from ethyl vinyl acetate or thermo-plastic elastomer, feel slimy, can be hard to get out of a bottle (let alone get back in if you don't finish the bottle in one go), are radically unrecyclable, but don't contaminate wines. I've heard rumours that they might draw pleasant flavours out of wines rather than putting unpleasant ones in, but even if true this would be a lesser evil; the wine would still be drinkable.

Never say 'never' where matters of technology are concerned, but for the time being it's hard to see plastic corks ever replacing true cork for fine wines intended for long storage and maturation in bottle, since the very slow 'breathing' which a wine is said to perform through its cork is not possible with plastic's tight seal. The ageing trajectory of such wines would be different. Would it be better? Only long-term experiments of several decade's duration will show.

Aesthetically, too, plastic corks don't strike quite the right note. Sinking a corkscrew into the deep, moist, yielding embrace of a long cork in a

well stored bottle, and then drawing it out of the
neck with a slow sigh, is a piece of theatre many of
us will not relinquish lightly.

38 Screwcaps and crown caps are just as good

And it doesn't stop there, either. After all, if you're
giving up on the idea of stuffing a little bit of tree
bark into the end of your bottle to keep the wine in,
why stuff a piece of plastic in there instead? Perhaps
the time for stuffing things in bottles is over.

The great advantage of the screwcap is that you
can throw your corkscrew away. In quality-control
tests, it performs adequately at least up to the 10-
year mark, keeping wines as fresh as real corks and
plastic corks. It's been used for a long-time for cheap
wines such as Liebfraumilch and Lambrusco, which
has given it a doubtful, park-bench image; the
Australians, in particular, are working hard to change
this by using screwcap closures on respectable and
even ambitious wines – though not, as yet (other
than for experimental purposes), on wines intended
for cellaring. Perhaps what's required is a different,
more aesthetically appealing form of screw cap.

Finally, why not use a crown cap or beer-bottle
top? You generally need a bottle opener for this
(though twist-off versions exist); it also suffers image-
problems as a closure for wine bottles; but it works
perfectly well as a secure, air-tight stopper for short
or mid-term storage. Almost every mouthful of
Champagne you've ever drunk, as it happens,
acquired its sparkle under crown caps before being
finished prior to sale with real corks – for, in most
cases, no more than cosmetic or aesthetic effect.

Part 4

The Glass: Tasting Wine

39 Wines have three elements

At last: let's get going on a few bottles. Before we start, though, a word about intent. You're reading this book because you enjoy wine, and you want to know a bit more about it. In other words, you're a drinker who would also like to be a taster. Drinking concerns the satisfaction of a particular type of appetite; tasting is about understanding and appreciating beauty expressed in scent and flavour. Drinkers of a coarse and philistine bent may view tasters as amusing or pretentious; tasters (who are, after all, also drinkers) know better. They're just getting their money's worth, and enjoying one of the world's great sensual pleasures.

All of that said, tasting can be an intensely private matter if you wish. All it requires is a little basic equipment and an open, observant mind. People do differ in their innate tasting abilities, but if you're reading this book at all, the chances are that you have the potential to become a good taster, since wine already means more to you than to most. (The tone deaf rarely read books on music; the flat-footed avoid dance classes.) Given the basic aptitude which you already have, you simply need experience, and you've got the rest of your life for that.

In order to analyse wine, all you have to do is concentrate on two groups of three elements.

The first tripartite group is obvious: appearance, scent and flavour. We separate the last two elements, because we 'smell' things before we put them in our mouths and 'taste' things afterwards, as we suck or chew; yet much of what we perceive to be taste is actually aroma. (This is why you can't 'taste' anything when a cold blocks your nose.) Even solid substances in the mouth rapidly become volatile liquids; their vapours pass up a back stairway between the mouth and the nose, called the retronasal passage. These vapours are registered by tiny olfactory hairs sitting in a bath of mucous fluid at the back of the nose; the hairs are prolongations of nerve fibres which are, in turn, connected to a part of the brain called the olfactory bulb. All your poor old taste buds do, down on the tongue, is measure four primary tastes: sweetness, acidity, bitterness and saltiness. A great palate *is* a great nose. Nonetheless we carry on dividing the pleasure of wine into appearance, aroma and flavour because we drink the stuff rather than snort it.

The second group of three elements is more useful for actually analysing a wine once it's in your mouth. If you do any cooking – vegetarians, look aside – you'll be used to cutting up dead animals (or bits of animals). What you're dealing with could usually be divided into bone, flesh and fat. Similarly, when you have a wine in your mouth, you can usually get a handle on three separate components: its acidity, its tannin or texture, and its richness or fullness.

All wines have some acidity and, since it's one of the four primary tastes, it's easy enough to spot.

All red wines and some white wines have tannin (see section 17), but every wine has a textural dimension, from very delicate and light through tough and chewy to unctuous and supple. This textural sensation is sometimes called 'mouthfeel'.

Richness or fullness of flavour is a slightly more difficult concept to grasp. It may include the sweetness of any residual sugar left in a wine, and will always include the sweetish warmth of flavour which comes from wine's alcohol component. (To see how vital a role alcohol, the *eminence grise* of wine, plays in its flavour, try low-alcohol or alcohol-free wines – they always seem shockingly thin.) Richness and fullness also include the huge range of extractive flavours a wine may include; these may remind you of fruits, or vegetables, or spices, or of almost anything else we are capable of apprehending with our sense of taste and smell.

Dividing a wine up into its three component parts in this way is a useful sorting exercise, and it can also begin pointing you in the direction of working out how successful or unsuccessful a wine is. All successful wines must possess a palpable harmony between these three components. Failed wines (and, on occasion, immature or over-aged wines) will show disharmony or imbalance – too much (or too little) acidity, for example, or an over-tough texture, or an inappropriate lack of richness or fullness of flavour. Great wines will not only present this harmony, but will sear it on to your mind (or olfactory bulb) with their intensity and concentration.

40 The best glasses are tulip-shaped

Unlike skiing, American football or wildlife photography, enjoying wine to the full requires only a few simple, affordable pieces of equipment. And here is the most important of them.

The glass perched on the edge of my computer tray is 6 inches tall, plain and uncut. The bowl is around four inches tall, with its widest point at its base. From there it tapers gently up to the rim, giving the bowl the appearance of a newly opened tulip. It's what's called an ISO glass (ISO stands for International Standards Organisation); it's designed both for wine-tasting and wine-drinking, and it costs around half the price of an inexpensive bottle from the nearest supermarket.

Let's charge it with wine.

Stop, stop: that's plenty. I know it looks mean at

first, only filling it one-third full – but no one said you can't have another helping. (And a third, and a fourth, if you want, and so on until the bottle is empty.)

The reason for the plain glass is now plain to see: that purple-red colour can be enjoyed in all its glory. It's the colour of fat, ripe blackberries basking under an opulent September sun. Tip the glass on to its side, and suddenly the wine begins to show you its spectrum: that heart of sombre, thunderstorm purple lightens to paeony red as the volume of wine thins, before finally losing itself in maroon-tinged pink out where the glass draws the lip of liquid upwards by surface tension (this is called, in winespeak, the meniscus). If you like cut glass or engraved glass – and I agree that, when candles are lit, the scintillations of wine through cut glass are delicious in themselves – then by all means use it. For analytical purposes, though, plain glass is best.

The colour of wine tells you much. Oaked white wines, for example, are nearly always fuller and more golden in colour than those that have passed their infancy in stainless steel. Very bright red wines are usually high in acidity; dull red wines tend to be low in acidity. Depth of colour, and the relative hue within the spectrum of black-purple to red-brown, is a major clue to a wine's age: the browner, the older.

The blenders of vintage port work very painstakingly with colour, since fractional graduations of extra depth in these already opaque black-purple wines promise quality and longevity. Just over a week ago, I attended a tasting of 28-year-old vintage ports (the 1970s), and colour was still giving the game away: the group of half-a-dozen darkest wines (Dow, Calem, Graham, Gould Campbell, Fonseca and Taylor, since you ask) were among the most impressive and satisfying in aroma and flavour terms, too.

From warm climates, depth of colour in young red wines often equates with ripeness and richness of flavour. With other wines, most notably red burgundies and wines made from the Pinot Noir grape variety, plus red wines in general made in cool climates, depth of colour can be deceptive, since the extraction required often means leaching out unpleasant as well as pleasant characters. Indeed I remember an English red wine, once – yes, they do exist, but wait for the end of the story – called Wellow. I looked twice when I first saw it, so dark and so bright was it; I leapt enthusiastically into the glass. Horror! The brightness was vertiginous acidity; the depth marked the extraction of every last flavour, a few of them ripe but most unripe, herbaceous and sour, that the surly English summer had communicated to the grapes. Alas, poor Wellow; it exists no more.

But why, you keep asking, only one-third full? Read on.

You've paid for aroma as well as flavour

In January of the year in which I write this, the Australian Wine Bureau in Britain organised a conference on the future of Australian wine. The day's biggest laugh came when David Combe of Southcorp, describing the new generation running Australia's small set of very large wine companies, pointed out that "businessmen with a proven record of driving successful businesses" were now at the helm, and no longer those people he described, with carefully targeted and playfully delivered contempt, as "corksniffers". The entire audience immediately rallied to the much-loved (and now beleaguered) cause of corksniffing, and later speakers fell over themselves to establish their corksniffing credentials. A nerve had been touched.

People who like wine like sniffing. They sniff their food; they sniff the air on moist autumn mornings; they sniff new clothes, old books, strange rooms. One way in which wine can play a vital civilizing role is that it can help restore to us the 'lost' sense of smell, and give the world an olfactory dimension which most are unaware of or, worse still, deliberately ignore. Wine teaches you to smell – to smell first, before anything else, and to dwell a while in what you find. Wine teaches you to read smells, and to learn from smells. Wine teaches you that beauty and ugliness of scent have repercussions, meanings, consequences, occasionally almost a moral force. The good winegrower creates beautiful scents; you can smell shortcuts and wasted opportunities in the lazy winemaker's sulphury wine.

Bad wine, at the very best, smells boring; good wine smells good. And one of the definitions of great wine is that it smells more beautiful than you would think any liquid could smell. A friend put a glass of white wine in front of me a month or two ago. We were in a restaurant, though he had brought all the bottles; we hadn't yet eaten. For a moment, it seemed as if the whole of the meal ahead of us had been concentrated into the aroma of this white wine: bread, butter, meat stock, wild mushrooms, a little bacon; finally honey, too, and nuts, with the memory of heady conservatory flowers. Above all, though, this was one scent, round and harmonious, endowed with an extraordinarily enticing beauty. Once smelled, you could not but drink. We were early, by the way; the restaurant was empty; they were still chopping things in the kitchen. How could any liquid surrender so much aroma as that bottle of Montrachet, a quarter of a century old?

This, finally, is a mystery; all I would like to impress upon you here is that, for every five pounds, dollars, francs, marks or roubles you spend on wine, at least one is for pure aroma, that ethereal and unbefuddling experience open to you before you put wine in your mouth.

Which, in the end, is why you shouldn't fill your glass more than a third full. You can then swirl the wine gently, which will help release its aromas; you can return to the wine numerous times over the course of an hour or two, and often find fascinatingly different forms of aromatic expression there. Wines speak two languages, and one is pure aroma. It's worth learning.

Tasting: have fun

Now, at long last, it's time for a taste. It's up to you exactly how this intimate matter is arranged; the main thing to avoid is simply sluicing the wine across the furrowed tongue and straight down the throat. Let the wine rest in the mouth, grow warm in the mouth, relax in the mouth; let it touch every part of the tongue. If you want to introduce some air in there, and work the wine around the mouth as you do so, that's fine, too, though it's not obligatory. As we discovered in section 40, much of the taste of wine is actually aroma; the purpose of these stratagems is not only to get the tongue to register every nuance of the four primary flavours – as well as the texture and temperature of a wine and any fizziness it may have – but also to render as much of the wine as volatile as possible, so that your olfactory hairs (and bulb) can experience it most intensely. Simply knocking wine back is to rob yourself of pleasure.

You may eventually find specific tasting techniques suit certain wines. For example, I like to taste (and drink) German Riesling wines with the tip of the tongue for as long as possible, before letting it back to flood the rest of the mouth. Sweetness is perceived at the tongue's tip, and acidity at its sides; the balance between the two elements is paramount in these featherweight wines. They thrill most when tasted in this way. Young vintage port demands the opposite approach. This is a wine so extravagantly multidimensional, so ferociously extractive and so fierily alcoholic that I find it has to be released, like a particularly dangerous prisoner, gently, on to the back of the tongue, before being allowed to flood the mouth from the back forwards, lashing out with its flavours of crushed vegetation, hammered stalks and spattered blackberries. That's what works for me, anyway; your mouth may be different. Experiment; lark about; have fun.

What you'll discover as you do so is that wine isn't a mansion of compartmentalised rooms, each closed and discrete, but more a kind of giant open-plan office. The number of conceivable flavours is enormous, and they all happily run and bump into each other – which is what makes blind tasting (guessing the identity of a wine by sensory means alone) so humiliatingly difficult. To prove the point, I'm inviting you to one right now.

43
Keep an open mind

There are four glasses of wine on the table. Have a go at them; we'll compare notes afterwards.

Glass one: pale green-white colour; orchard-fresh scent of juicy grapes and citrus peels; lively, gossamer-light flavour with no detectable alcohol, and high-definition, crisp-edged flavours of crunchy apples and grapefruit with a zesty mineral finish. Mouth-shiveringly good – but am I sure it's not just fruit juice?

Glass two: clear, light garnet red, with a little tile-red towards the rim, and soft insinuating aromas of fawn and calf-skin and roses; light but strangely penetrating currenty flavours, with a decidedly meaty edge. Seems to swell and expand in the mouth, acquiring flesh. Great harmony, yet poised and fresh, too. One sip dictates another. Pure wine.

Glass three: rich, amber-gold colour, with an extraordinary scent of wet straw, cheese and limes. Massive, intense, rapier-like flavour of absolute dryness, with a deep tongue-slicing edge; lingers in the mouth for minutes, recollecting heat and lemons. How can wine be this intense? It almost hurts to sip.

Glass four: black. Thick and unctuous, very nearly a spooning texture; intense, cloying scent of raisins and figs. Syrup-thick on the tongue, and intensely sweet, like a kind of raisin essence. Undrinkable but monumental. Should be turned into tablets and supplied to polar explorers.

Extraordinary, eh?

The contents of the four glasses are so different that it's hard to believe they're all called 'wine'. The second glass, of course, corresponds to what most of us would like to sit down with on most evenings: dry red (or white) wine for food, especially when it can acquire such referential complexity and devastating grace. The other wines expand our horizons – if we let them.

Every time you open a bottle, prepare for the unexpected. Treat a bottle of wine like a child or a stranger, with sympathy and an open mind: how does it express itself? What is it conveying or suggesting? In what ways is it beautiful or memorable? I don't mean you should be uncritical, and faulty or failed wines will soon disappoint, but preconceived notions of what wines should or shouldn't taste like will quickly obscure a beauty which might otherwise have brought pleasure. Don't dismiss any wine until you've tried it.

So you want to know what you've just tasted? The first wine was a young white Riesling wine from the Mosel valley in Germany, with all of eight per cent alcohol ; the second was a 25-year-old red burgundy from the perfectly sited Grand Cru vineyard of Chambertin. The third wine was a 1910 vintage Madeira made from the Sercial grape variety; the fourth was a fortified wine made from Pedro Ximenez grapes in the sherry region. Come back tomorrow and we could taste four more, just as different from each other as these were.

Wines can disappoint

Everything great, then? Wine the key to sensual bliss, geographical poignancy and universal happiness?

Alas no. Let's be honest: wine can often be bitterly frustrating and disappointing. No one knows this better than wine writers: professional enthusiasts, in other words, who constantly trumpet their recommendations to the world at large, and seem to spend their lives surfing a wave of multi-orgasmic gustatory delirium. Far from being (as they might appear) serenely confident, wine writers are often convulsed with doubt and uncertainty. They know full well that one man's 'zingy, grassy

Sauvignon' might be another's 'thin, weedy white',
and that twelve bottles from even the same case of
wine might each exhibit fractional or not-so-
fractional variations that will cause consumers to
question not only their professional competence but
their mental health and the marital status of their
mothers at the moment of their birth.

There are two main sources of frustration in
wine (faults aside – which we'll deal with in the next
section). These could be summarised as "Not as good
as I hoped," and "Not as good as last time".

"Not as good as I hoped" covers several sorts of
situation. You might have read a mouthwatering
description of a particular type of wine (pungent,
fresh, cherry-kernel-charged Valpolicella Classico,
let's say), and then gone out to buy one and found it
thin, acidic and aspirin-like; or you might have
bought a specific writer's recommendation from a
newspaper ("Dupont's 1999 Old-Vines Carignan Vin
de Pays d'Oc from Sainsway at £3.99 is bursting with
ripe damson fruit and chocolate depth") and found it
... thin, acidic and aspirin-like.

The first problem here is that not all producers
make memorable and authentic examples of regional
styles. Whether we're talking about Bordeaux or the
Barossa, there are always good, bad and indifferent
winemakers. It is in sorting out the talented goats
from the talentless sheep that wine journalists and
their recommendations come into their own.

The second problem is the universal one of
subjectivity: my damsons may be your aspirins. The
only solution here, if you're regularly disappointed, is
to change your supplier of recommendations. In the
great democracy of taste, there are no rights and
wrongs, only differences.

"Not as good as last time" is even more difficult
to solve. The moment you empty a big bucket of
wine into twelve different bottles, you create twelve

different wines. The more the years roll by, the more different these twelve wines will become. Wine is inherently inconsistent and variable – as, of course, are the circumstances under which you drink wines. You may take a holiday on the French Atlantic coast, you may sit down to a dozen oysters within view of the sea, and you may think the bottle of Gros Plant the cheery restaurateur offers you a wonderfully pungent and racy wine. He gives you the grower's address, you go off and buy a couple of bargain cases, and life seems wonderful. Get it back home, sip it with steak-and-kidney pie on the first snowy night of winter, and I guarantee you'll revise your opinion. The circumstances, here, are hugely different, but it also happens (as wine writers know all too well) that on some days even average wines taste memorable and on other days even grand wines taste mealy. Inconsistency in the mouth is as real as inconsistency in the bottle.

Finally, even the greatest wines go through phases and one of them is, unfortunately, adolescence. Sumptuously appealing, deep-fruited classics can become surly and taciturn after a few years, to the extent that you may consider losing patience with them and throwing them out at the nearest auctioneer. Persist, though, and you may find the magic returns, subtly transfigured into something still more seductive and eloquent than before. Some wines, indeed, seem to turn their charm on and off in a completely unsystematic way, regardless of any putative adolescence. Infuriating.

Be prepared for setbacks and disappointments, then. Wine, I'm tempted yet again to say, is only human.

45
Bad or 'off' wine is rare

While we're still in the mood of bleak realism
generated by the last section, we might as well
accept that, not only will some bottles disappoint us,
but others will seem downright disgusting. The
dividing line between that which is subjectively
unpleasant and that which is objectively faulty is, in
practice, relatively easy for most of us to establish;
you can drink the former, albeit with subdued
pleasure, while the latter is undrinkable.

Fortunately, faulty wines are uncommon. If we
exclude corkiness (see section 36), which can afflict
as many as one in twenty bottles, regular wine-
drinkers are likely to encounter a faulty bottle no
more than once every year or two.

All these faults can be seen or smelled: there's
no need to put the wine in your mouth. You probably
won't want to, anyway. Examples of faults which can
be seen include hazy or cloudy wines, generally due
to micro-organisms; and wines which should be still
but appear to be fizzy, due to an unwanted secondary
fermentation or malolactic fermentation in bottle.
Many wines, note, are deliberately bottled with a
little extra CO_2 to keep them fresh, so don't assume
that a prickle of gas is necessarily a fault. If the gas is
caused by a fault, the wine will generally not smell
fresh or clean.

The formation of sediment is, in almost all
cases, a natural (if occasionally inconvenient) process,
and generally indicates that a wine has not been
excessively fined or filtered – a good sign, in other
words. Indeed I'm disappointed and mildly suspicious
if any medium-bodied or full-bodied red wine
originally costing £10 or more does not, after a
decade in my cellar, throw a palpable sediment: if it's
good, it should. If there has been any accompanying
bacteriological spoilage, this will be evident in the

wine's aroma, which will be rank or dirty.

Corkiness aside, the four main wine faults, all of them detectable with a sniff, are volatile acidity, oxidation, sulphur spoilage and cask faults. The first two are examples of traits which, in barely detectable amounts, can add to a wine's complexity and subtlety but which, when substantially evident, can ruin a wine.

Volatile acidity is measured by the amount of acetic acid in a wine, but detected by its levels of volatile ethyl acetate: the smell is sharp, piquant, 'high-toned', pear-droppy, solvent-like; the taste is acidic. If you're noticing it, the level is too high.

Oxidation is the opposite: flat, stale, tired and dull are the kind of words which will spring to mind when you sniff an oxidised wine. The colour of the wine will probably be browner and more lacklustre than it should be and, if you press on and taste the wine, you'll find it hard and uninspiring.

Sulphur spoilage is the easiest of all to spot: the wine stinks. Hydrogen sulphide smells in wine vary from relatively acceptable leathery or farmyardy smells through uncomfortable 'smelly sock' scents to unacceptable smells of rotten eggs or intestinal gas; mercaptans (derived from hydrogen sulphide) are worse still: decaying, rancid, putrid.

Free sulphur (sulphur which has not combined with any other chemical component in the wine) is very different: it provides a physical shock to the nose and, sometimes, the lungs, and can trigger asthma attacks. Excessive amounts of free sulphur tend to be found in young white wines containing residual sugar: it's all-too-common a fault in German wines in general.

Finally, the greatly increased use of small oak barrels in winemaking over the last two decades has resulted in more wines showing faults attributable to poor cask quality (especially inadequately seasoned wood) and maintenance (bacteriological spoilage). Cask problems tend to spoil the aroma of wine in a similar way to corkiness, giving it musty, mouldy, dank, mushroomy, cardboardy aromas.

If you can, you should always return a faulty wine to whoever sold it to you, so that he or she in turn can take the problem up with the supplier; this includes problems of corkiness. In restaurants, too, always refuse wines which smell bad. It's a hassle, I agree, since the waiter or the shop assistant may well be less interested in wine, and less sensitive to its nuances, than you are. If you are very badly treated, try writing to a wine journalist; we're always interested!

46 Discussing wines: don't be shy

If you've read this far, then it's a fair bet that you like wine. Maybe you live on your own in a granite tower on a desolate, windswept peninsula accessible only by a skilfully navigated rowing boat and thus drink all your best bottles in meditative isolation, but somehow I think it's unlikely. More probably you drink wine with a partner and, occasionally, have a few more friends round to share some bottles. In either case, sooner or later you're going to want to talk about the wines you're drinking. And then you'll want words. Which ones?

This is a surprisingly controversial issue. The controversy arises because human beings have been lazy about developing a vocabulary of taste. If I tell you I'm wearing a blue jumper, brown trousers and a black tie, you will immediately be able to visualize my general appearance. It is simply not possible to describe three tastes in as straightforward a way. I have to borrow terms for other taste sensations and use them analogically: a blackcurranty Chilean Cabernet, a creamy white burgundy, a zesty New Zealand Sauvignon. (Imagine, correspondingly, that we didn't have a vocabulary for colour. I would have to say I'm wearing a cornflower jumper, earthy trousers and a night-like tie.) The vocabulary problem is still more evidence that we've neglected our senses of smell and taste in favour of our sense of sight, hearing and touch.

Most wine descriptions fall into either conservative or radical camps, and there are sometimes strong feelings of hostility between the two. Conservatives think that all wines just taste of wine, and differentiate between them by using simple terms for texture and weight like 'full-bodied' and 'light-bodied', and evaluative terms like 'lovely' or 'disappointing' (or even, for sarcastic purposes, 'presumptuous'). Fair enough, but such descriptions quickly become dull and repetitive, and do not even begin to convey what a wine actually tastes like to someone who hasn't tasted it.

Radicals take the opposite tack: they snatch analogies from the sensual world around us in order to convey, with as much vividness as possible, what a wine tastes like. Indeed some wine descriptions have gone so far down the path of analogical delirium as to become, justifiably, the butt of popular humour. You know the kind of thing I mean: "Wow! When I smell this wine I get the countryside, I get autumn, I get heat, I get piles of leathery, sweaty gymshoes in a wheelbarrow being pushed through a soup of crushed blackberries!" Not all radical wine descriptions are useful, accurate or carefully composed, but when they are, they are the only means open to us to convey the taste of a wine to another human being who hasn't experienced it. Just remember they aren't meant literally. No one is suggesting that Chilean Cabernet contains blackcurrants instead of grapes, or that white burgundy has had cream added to it. Those terms are employed because they are the only linguistic means we have of describing the *type* of taste Chilean Cabernet has or white burgundy has.

When you're describing a wine to someone else, then, don't be shy. Let yourself go; let your imagination roam; ransack your sensual memory for those distant but vivid triggers which will help you share the pleasure of wine with your friends. It's all fun, after all, and the only goal is vivid communication.

47
A little dictionary of wine terms

First of all, please accept my sympathy. I remember how confusing wine-tasting terms seemed to me at first. What on earth did 'fruit' mean in relation to wine, for example? Fruit? Mounds of apples, piles of tangerines, bunches of bananas? Whaaaaat?

After a while, believe me, it does fit into place. I recall the first time I understood the term 'buttery' about a white Chardonnay, for example. Someone gave me a glass of Montagny from an average vintage, about six years old, and – there it was. A scent I recognized as being just like the butter you'd melt in the pan before making scrambled eggs. From then on, I knew what 'buttery' meant in relation to wine; I'd got a fix on it. And, one by one, all the other keys have followed – as they will for you, provided that you keep drinking, tasting and thinking.

In the following mini-dictionary, I've concentrated on defining the vaguer, more general terms, rather than self-explanatory triggers like 'grassy', 'plummy', 'oaky' and so on.

acid All wines need some acidity; how much, though, and of what sort? Acid is the most prominent of the three fundamental balancing elements in wine and, in my opinion, a critical factor in wine quality. Look for, taste and analyse the acidity in all wines, and use this as the starting point for your judgement of them. There is no recipe, and great wines can have high (Saar Riesling) or low (Bordeaux from warm vintages) acid levels. Whatever the level, though, the acidity must be natural, ripe and appealing in some way or other, and it must be satisfactorily balanced in relation to the whole wine.

alcohol The canvas on which wine is painted. As with acid, the level varies and is not in itself important: what matters is the overall balance and harmony in the wine. Alcohol should neither obtrude, making a wine 'hot' and heavy, nor be deficient, making it thin, empty and slight.

balance The fundamental concept within wine appreciation, and something that all good or great wines must possess: harmony between their component parts.

blind tasting One in which the identity of the wines tasted is unknown. Blind tasting is essential for making critical comparisons between wines.

body The perceived weight of a wine in the mouth.

chewy Amply and palpably textured, but not rough or harsh.

complex Used to describe wines which seem to contain many finely nuanced flavours.

creamy Smooth, soft and unctuous, sometimes (especially white wines) with lactic-like flavours derived from contact with yeast lees.

dense Used to describe wines which have both concentration of flavour and textural depth.

earthy Used of wines which seem to taste of soil or minerals. A common component of European wines, sometimes at the expense of fruit flavours.

extract The dry residue left by wine after all the liquid has evaporated.

finish The final flavours of a wine, left after you swallow.

fresh Clean, bright and lively, often with high acid levels, clear fruit flavours, and sometimes with green or grassy overtones.

fruit As a general term, used of that element of a wine's flavour which suggests kinship with any fruit. Many New World wines are said to be 'fruit-driven', meaning that fruit flavours occupy their foreground, and perhaps account for all of their flavour.

green Used to describe vegetal or herbaceous aromas or flavours in general.

grippy Used to describe a wine whose tannins seem, Velcro-like, to seize the tongue.

hot Used to describe clumsy, loose-knit wines, often with high and unbalanced alcohol levels and poor fruit definition.

intense Used to describe a larger-than-average volume of flavour within a wine. Most great wines are intense, but not all intensely flavoured wines are great, since intensity can be created by artificial additives like acid.

jammy A style of fruit flavour which is vague, lacks definition and seems 'hot', as simmering jam does.

juicy Vigorous, vivid and youthful style of fruit flavour within a wine.

length The amount of time during which a wine's flavour seems to linger in the mouth.

mouthfeel Technical term used to describe the textural nature of a wine.

richness Used to describe in general the wealth and fullness of flavour a wine may possess, as distinct from its acidity and its tannin or textural component. Richly flavoured wines can be dry; this term does not necessarily imply sweetness.

rough Unpleasantly abrasive in flavour or texture,

due to imbalanced acids and tannins and, often, a lack of richness.

round Soft-contoured in flavour, without sharpness or angular edges.

smooth Used of a wine whose texture is barely palpable, supple and sometimes glycerous (reminiscent of the slippery texture of glycerine).

soft Used of a wine whose texture is fine-grained, giving an impression of gentleness and, often, roundedness.

spicy Used to describe a wine which might (often due to ageing in new French oak) suggest spices like cinnamon or clove, but also more generally to describe a range of exotic wine aromas and flavours which do not suggest fruit, earth or animal notes.

structure The way in which and degree to which a wine is internally joined, made evident in analytical tasting by examination of its component flavours and textures.

tannin The textural element of wine, derived from grape skins – therefore most evident in red wines.

tight Used of a wine, often young, whose flavour elements are discernible yet close-knit, and have not yet acquired harmony and articulacy.

vinous A difficult term to grasp at first, this signifies the 'winey' component of wine: distinctive yet subtle post-fermentation flavours which help give a wine sinew and structure. For example, what distinguishes most white burgundy from most international Chardonnay, for me, is vinosity. Not widely acknowledged within New World winemaking: Australia's Brian Croser once defined vinosity to me as 'absence of fruit flavour'.

Part 5

The Shop: Buying Wine

48 Wine is chaotic

It's best to know the bad news first, so … welcome to chaos, on an interplanetary scale. Argue if you wish, but I'd suggest there is no single product human beings can buy which is more diverse, more confusing, more fluctuating, more unpredictable, more unfathomable and finally more unknowable than wine. It is the final frontier of commercial anarchy. The 'brand', that homogenising totem of commerce, is a laughably weak concept in the wine world. Wine, once again, reflects life in its pullulating diversity; that is its joy.

And, for consumers, its curse. So many place names, so many vintages, so many grape varieties, so many producers: you may think you're alone in suffering from bottle vertigo in a wine shop or supermarket, but even the so-called 'experts' (me, for example) get dizzy when confronted by those tightly stacked shelves, too. The basic data bank is huge, and every year it gets thoroughly revised and expanded.

This will never change. I've long since accepted that I'll never 'know everything' about wine, and that the best I can hope for is a passing familiarity with a few transient zones in the grand gallery.

The situation is not hopeless, though: there is a way forward. You could call it a two-point plan. We'll start in the next section with point one; point two comes in section 67. And, as you go, you may find that you know more than you think.

49 Grape varieties first

Let's imagine a perfect world. There would be four ways in which you could, eventually, come to 'know everything' about wine. You could first learn what each grape variety tasted like, then you could set about discovering how wines from every geographical region performed. Next you could gauge how good at their job all the wine producers in the world were; and finally you could make an assessment of how successful all the different vintages had ever been. Perfect – but, of course, impossible.

Now let's go back to the real, imperfect world. Of those four avenues of knowledge, the easiest to stroll down is the Avenue of Grape Varieties. Sure, there are thousands of them, and you'll never wrap your tongue round the lot; but most wines on our shop shelves, as we discovered back in section 4, are made from just two dozen or so. If you can get a fix on those two dozen in your sensory memory, you're already well on the way towards having some idea about how a particular wine might taste. That, therefore, is where we will begin our shopping plan.

There's only one fat fly in the ointment. This is the fact that most major European wine regions don't use grape variety names for their top wines (those for which demarcated areas exist). Such wines tend to be labelled with the name of their regions alone. As often as not, too, they are made from a blend of grape varieties rather than a single, sensorially recognizable variety. Here, therefore, is a reference key to help you understand which key European wine names equate with particular grape varieties. (If you want more detail, buy Jancis Robinson's little paperback *Guide to Wine Grapes*, published in Britain by Oxford University Press, and immediately turn to the useful section at the end of the book called 'The Grapes Behind The Names'. This lists all the grapes permitted for a large range of European regionally demarcated wines.)

Cabernet Sauvignon: used in blends with Merlot and small proportions of other varieties in Bordeaux and its sub-appellations, including Haut-Médoc, Médoc, St Estèphe, Pauillac, St Julien, Margaux, Moulis, Listrac, Pessac-Léognan, Graves, Côtes de Bourg, Côtes de Blaye. Also used in Buzet, Bergerac and smaller appellations of south-west France.

Pinot Noir: used for red burgundy (Bourgogne Rouge) and for all Burgundy's numerous red-wine appellations, including Santenay, Volnay, Pommard, Beaune, Aloxe-Corton, Nuits-St-Georges, Vosne-Romanée, Clos de Vougeot, Chambolle-Musigny, Morey-St-Denis, Gevrey-Chambertin, Fixin, Mercurey and Givry. Pinot Noir, made as a white wine, is one of Champagne's three main grape varieties.

Merlot: used in blends with Cabernet Sauvignon, Cabernet Franc and small proportions of other varieties in sub-appellations of Bordeaux, including St Emilion, Pomerol, Lalande-de-Pomerol, Lussac-, Montagne-, St Georges- and Puisseguin-St-Emilion, Côtes de Castillon, Côtes de Bourg, Côtes de Blaye and Graves.

Cabernet Franc: used in Loire valley red wine appellations like Saumur-Champigny, Bourgueil, St Nicolas de Bourgeuil, Chinon, Anjou-Villages, as well as in blends with Merlot and Cabernet Sauvignon in most Bordeaux appellations, and particularly St-Emilion, Pomerol and Fronsac. Also called Bouchet and Breton.

Syrah/Shiraz: used in Northern Rhône red-wine appellations like Côte Rôtie, Hermitage, Crozes-Hermitage, St Joseph and Cornas, as well as in some Côtes du Rhône; also used as a blending variety in Southern Rhône appellations like Châteauneuf-du-Pape, and in Languedoc appellations like Coteaux du Languedoc, Costières du Nîmes, Côtes du Roussillon and -Villages, Faugères, Fitou, Minervois and St Chinian.

Grenache/Garnacha: used as a blending grape in Southern Rhône appellations like Châteauneuf-du-Pape, Gigondas, Vacqueyras, Tavel, Lirac and Côtes du Rhône, and in Languedoc appellations such as Coteaux du Languedoc, Corbières, Minervois, Costières de Nîmes, Côtes du Roussillon and -Villages, Faugères, Fitou and St Chinian; used as a blending grape throughout Spain, but especially in Rioja, Navarra and Priorato.

Sangiovese: used as the principal grape variety for the various Chianti wines, Brunello and Rosso di Montalcino, Vino Nobile di Montepulciano, Torgiano, Montefalco, Rosso Piceno and as a blending grape in other Italian DOCs (DOC stands for Denominazione di Origine Controllata) and in France's Corsica (as Nielluccio). Also called Sangioveto, Brunello and Morellino.

Nebbiolo: used as the principal grape variety for Barolo, Barbaresco, Valtellina Superiore, Gattinara, Ghemme, Carema and some other small North Italian DOCs. Also called Spanna.

Tempranillo: used as the principal grape variety for Rioja, Navarra, Ribera del Duero, Valdepeñas, Toro, Costers del Segre and Utiel-Requena, and as a blending grape in many other DOs (DO stands for Denominación de Origen). Also called Cencibel, Ull de Llebre, Ojo de Liebre, Tinto Fino and Tinto Aragonez. In Portugal it is called Tinta Roriz and in Argentina Tempranilla.

Chardonnay: used for white burgundy (Bourgogne Blanc) and for all Burgundy's numerous white-wine appellations, including the Chablis appellations, Chassagne-Montrachet, Puligny-Montrachet, Meursault, Rully, Montagny, the Mâcon appellations, Pouilly-Fuissé, -Loché and -Vinzelles, St Véran and

Beaujolais Blanc, and as one of the three main blending varieties in Champagne.

Sauvignon Blanc: used in Sancerre, Pouilly-Fumé, Quincy, Reuilly and Menetou-Salon, and as a blending variety in white Bordeaux, Pessac-Léognan, Graves, Barsac, Sauternes, Entre-Deux-Mers, Cadillac, Loupiac, Ste Croix-du-Mont, Bergerac, Buzet, Montravel, Monbazillac and other smaller appellations in south-west France.

Chenin Blanc: used for the white wines of the central Loire valley, such as Vouvray, Anjou, Savennières, Saumur, Bonnezeaux, Coteaux de l'Aubance, Coteaux du Layon, Jasnières, Montlouis and Quarts de Chaume. Also called Pineau de la Loire and (in South Africa) Steen.

Sémillon: used as a blending variety in white Bordeaux, Pessac-Léognan, Graves, Barsac, Sauternes, Entre-Deux-Mers, Cadillac, Loupiac, Ste Croix-du-Mont, Bergerac, Buzet, Montravel, Monbazillac and other smaller appellations in south-west France.

50
Cabernet Sauvignon: his nibs

There's an indefinable grandeur to Cabernet Sauvignon. Among red grape varieties, it's the one whose cheekbones are a little more prominent than everybody else's, whose head is held a little higher, whose back is a little straighter, and whose dark and distant eyes have the calm assurance of authority. Maybe you don't warm to it immediately; maybe you don't find it as sexy as Pinot Noir or Syrah; maybe its occasional severities and hauteurs exasperate you. Yet it's consistent at all levels; and at the top level few varieties can rival it for intricately layered, multifaceted complexity. How strange, then, that its Mum should be the faintly vulgar Sauvignon Blanc and its Dad the occasionally weedy Cabernet Franc. There's no accounting for genetics.

It's usually considered the leading red-wine variety of Bordeaux. In fact, Merlot is more widely planted there, yet because Cabernet Sauvignon is dominant in the plantings of the great estates of the Médoc (whose wines were traditionally more widely exported than those from the much smaller properties of St-Emilion and Pomerol) it has become known as the Bordeaux variety. Bordeaux Cabernet remains the ideal for the rest of the world: mid-weight, with the fine fresh balance which makes for great drinking, and with a remarkable ability to age and to acquire layers of allusiveness as it does so. It has a distinctly blackcurranty quality, yet its flavour is never merely fruity; there always seems to be an extra dimension of flavoury refinement which can remind the drinker of lead pencils, cedar and (from the Graves and Pessac-Léognan) a caressing, textured earthiness. When young, it has a vivid pungency of flavour, and its ample tannins give the best Bordeaux Cabernet a densely woven, finely cut overcoat that only a spell in the cellar can slide away from the wine. With that dark age, it becomes more rich and yielding than you would have thought possible, with a soft choiceness of fruit and a meaty, tobacco-like fragrance. At best, that is: the worst Bordeaux Cabernet, by contrast, is thin, bony and reedy, like a failing, underconfident, cut-rate tenor in a provincial opera house.

Almost every serious wine-producing country has distinguished Cabernet to offer. Elsewhere in Europe, examples vary from Bulgaria's once-famous but now rather faded soft, curranty, soupy Cabernet to the deep, typically brooding examples of the most ambitious producers in Italy and Spain. In terms of sheer muscle and flesh, few can rival the best from California's Napa valley: these are tongue-pounding red wines of beefy power, high alcohol and deep drifts of fruit (often more bilberry or blackberry than blackcurrant). You sense, sometimes, that the winemaker's chief struggle was to rein everything back: the Napa's generous climate seems to give the wine almost too many dimensions for natural balance. Ordinary California Cabernet, by contrast, can lack intensity, and there are many graduations between the two extremes, sometimes with marked spice or eucalyptus notes.

For purity of blackcurrant fruit, Chilean Cabernet is unmatched. These are generally wines of simple but sometimes overwhelming deliciousness, so much so that a broad smile and a second sip is the only response. Argentina's Cabernet has a denser, more savoury quality but lacks the lyrical fruit intensity of Chilean examples.

Cabernet Sauvignon from Australia, like that from California, offers the drinker almost too wide a range to generalise about. The simplest Australian Cabernets (at all price ranges) are dark, relatively smooth, with obviously blackcurranty flavours lent a vanilla-and-mint sheen by oak or oak chips. They're like ice cream: seductive but stultifying. More ambitious examples, including many from the Coonawarra district, are less obviously fruity in flavour, hugely tannic and intense, yet with inappropriate acidity levels – which succeed in giving them both monotony and a rather frightening fierceness of flavour which time in the cellar will not necessarily mellow. Other, more successful, examples have a remarkable softness and expressivity, with distinctive overtones of tar, salt, earth and eucalyptus, and black profundity of fruit flavour.

It's hard to ripen Cabernet fully in New Zealand, thus many examples have herbaceous, green-capsicum flavours and lack wealth and width. When fully ripe, though, Kiwi Cabernet can produce a passable imitation of Bordeaux: dark wines with brisk, fresh, curranty flavours, ample svelte tannins, and a pencilly or stony edge to their flavours.

South Africa is moving away from the tough, stalky, green, hard and fruitless examples of the past towards Cabernets with an excitingly roasty style of ripeness, combined with poise and freshness – vivid yet full.

Let's sum up, then: blackcurrant fruit, palpable structure, occasional sternness, habitual poise and intermittent surges of intensity. That's Cabernet.

51 Pinot Noir: the wings of the dove

Pinot Noir is the romantic poet among red grape varieties. The rest of them get on with their work in a serious and consistent manner, compete with each other more or less on the same terms, and speak a common language of success or failure. Pinot, by contrast, is outrageously inconsistent, fickle and temperamental, as well as being very choosy about where it grows. When it succeeds, however (which it does in an original, unique and rule-breaking way), its charm is such that it reduces even its sternest critics to adulatory jelly. They forgive and forget – until the next disgraceful episode.

Red burgundy is the archetype, for better or worse. Its colour, even in youth, is a true garnet red rather than the black-red or purple-red of other varieties; sometimes the greatest burgundy can seem alarmingly light, while sombre depth and density of colour in a red burgundy can indicate an unbalanced, over-extracted wine. It should have the kind of soaring, enchanting and haunting scent that makes you want to use the word 'perfume', though there is a wide range of possibilities for exactly what that perfume suggests – cherries, plums, violets, beetroot, liquorice; later game and fur, forest undergrowth, wild mushrooms, even decaying flesh. And in the mouth it should strike the same soaring, lyrical note, quickly tumbling over itself as its fruit notes seem to gather power and breadth and allusiveness and take to the air, in the same way that the few wistful trumpet notes of 'The Last Post' can manage, reverberatively, amid the mists of November, to summon up the pathos and wretchedness and heroism of war. No other wine, in success, can so exceed the sum of its parts; no other wine can seem in analysis so slight, yet in impact and effect so powerful and magisterial.

It doesn't, in truth, do this very often outside France, and it does it rarely enough at home. Much red bugundy – dammit, most red burgundy – is just a light, sharp, thinnish, redcurranty red with a dry, tart finish. Supermarket burgundies, in particular, tend to be excruciatingly poor in quality; buy burgundy, above all, from a specialist.

Who else makes good Pinot? There are little pockets in most winegrowing countries (like Dealul Mare in Romania or Somontano in Spain) where light, sound, cherry-round reds can do the variety justice. California, strangely enough, can do rather better than that, perhaps because it has some of the most single-minded, Pinot-dreaming, site-researching fanatics in the world among its winegrowers: these are light yet glycerous, properly perfumed, vividly articulate reds, which swell the fruit range into plum and raspberry (as a warm year in Burgundy does) and provide typically spicy, liquorice back-notes, albeit over a rather creamier ground than at home in Beaune. Pay over £10 and you'll get far more consistent quality with Pinot from California than you will from Burgundy. Oregon's Pinots are successful, too, though less reliably so: they tend to be fresher and brisker than California's (more Burgundian, for better and worse).

New Zealand (and especially its Martinborough region) looks like another Pinot Noir natural: audacious depths of fruit, here, but without losing the variety's natural poise and finesse. Successes in Chile (pure cherry fruit, again, though lighter) are rare, but exist. I am unconvinced by Australia and South Africa's Pinot crusaders, since their wines seem, at present, to succeed through winery craft more than vineyard expression. Despite being satisfying in many ways (both countries can turn in deep Pinots with an ease Burgundians would envy), they lack the dove-winged, soaring essence.

Finally, of course, Pinot Noir, made as a white wine, is a crucial component in most Champagne blends – and hence in ambitious sparkling wines the world over. It brings depth and structure to such blends, and waves at the drinker with what it best described as a 'rooty' scent and flavour.

52 Merlot: the soft underbelly

If Cabernet is Don Quixote, Merlot is Sancho Panza; if Cabernet is Don Giovanni, Merlot is Leporello. Charm, softness, roundness, good humour, earthiness, voluptuousness – a red to unwind with, a red to joke with, a red to chew the fat with. And a red with plenty of fat of its own: that's Merlot.

Or the Merlot ideal. This is firmly founded on the wines of the Pomerol and St Emilion districts of Bordeaux, where Merlot is the kingpin, producing plummy, creamy reds of supple textures and brimming, cake-rich fruit. It is no accident that, over the last two decades, Bordeaux's most globally prized wines have been made chiefly from Merlot in these districts. Their appeal is direct and sensual, easy to understand yet nuanced and allusive, too. The Cabernet-dominated wines of the Médoc may form Bordeaux's aristocratic head, but Merlot in St Emilion and Pomerol constitutes its warm, peasant heart.

Merlot is relatively easy to grow, which means that both in Bordeaux and around the world it is more widely planted than Cabernet Sauvignon. Yet ask most wine drinkers to describe the taste of each, and they'd find the Cabernet photo-fit much easier to construct than Merlot's. Once it packs its bags and sets off on its travels, Merlot seems to lose its personality as easily as tourists lose banknotes stuffed into open handbags.

In Italy, it grows thin and weak. In California, it grows stern and tough. In Australia and South Africa and Bulgaria and Languedoc, it becomes just another red – the red Chardonnay, if you like. (California grower Randall Grahm, the wine world's punster-in-chief, brands the Merlot epidemic 'Merlotnoma'.) Even in Chile, whose national profile for red wines is remarkably close to Merlot's own, tickle-my-tummy style of playfulness and pleasure, it has yet to emerge as more than a dark and comely wine of easy virtue with lots below but little up top.

These are all generalities, and you will of course find Merlots in most of these countries which support the flesh-pot ideal with wines of structure, density and nascent complexity of flavour. (There's more than a few in America's Washington State, for example, or in Australia's Coonawarra.) As yet, though, they're the exception. Buy an ordinary bottle of Merlot and, for the time being, you can't expect to do any more than take a walk on the soft side.

53
Cabernet Franc: a shower in the woods

Spring is well underway as you step into the copse: the trees seethe with green. The ground seems almost to squeak as you walk over the fleshy leaves of the bulbs so recently hidden under winter's carapace, like tiny vegetative landmines. There's a stream winding its way through the tangle of fallen trees, moss and bushes; stagnant at summer's end, just now it's clean, gurgling and cressy. As you stand looking around you, a shower shakes itself down through the green and closing canopy above; the sudden weight of water seems, then, to spatter scent up out of the warming earth, out of the sprawl of living and dying wood.

I don't know why, but this is the kind of experience a glass of Cabernet Franc reminds me of. Freshness is the heart of its pleasure: a dark red in which juicy acidity is perhaps the dominant element, supported by extracts and richness of a brisk, let's-get-out-for-a-walk kind of constitution. It is, if you like, Merlot's antithesis: slim, nimble and sprightly rather than fat, rich and lazy.

I'm thinking, chiefly, of Cabernet Franc from the central part of the Loire valley, from Anjou, Chinon, Bourgeuil and Saumur. And I'm thinking of successful examples, too; unsuccessful ones can be horribly harsh and sour. Cabernet Franc is also widely grown in Bordeaux, but in general acts there as a complexing element in the symphonic blends for which that region is best known. Where it does come to the fore – in a sub-region called Fronsac and, most famously, in a grand wine called Cheval Blanc – you get less green woodland freshness and a range of deeper, fuller flavours: currants and raspberries shadowed by the memory of dark chocolate.

You will see wines labelled Cabernet Franc from other regions and countries but, in most cases, the variety is still too new in the ground to have really proved itself. In many cases, too, it has been planted simply to duplicate 'the Bordeaux blend', without being suited to the hot climates to which it is exposed. I have tried a couple of good'uns from South Africa and Australia, though, and found them dark, serious and well defined, leaving a black-chocolate wake behind their early-plum fruit. The exception to this rule of scarcity is Northern Italy, where Cabernet Franc has been living the expat life for a while, and where familiarity has all too often bred contempt. Expect, in most cases, no more than a cool and grassy quaffer.

54 Syrah/Shiraz: hot licks

Now here's a coming grape, a grape of ambition, a grape on the make. Very dapper, it is, in that sheeny suit, with those night-dark eyes and that swept-back Sorrento hair. There's often a faint intimation of burning rubber left hanging in the air as its nimble red sports car lurches to a halt. And then Syrah steps forward to hand you a bunch of flowers, too ...

France's northern Rhône valley is its home. There, it produces dark, sturdily constructed yet profoundly aromatic wines; wines that, when young, smell of flowers and cream, rubber and pepper, and which, when aged, retain the sense of creamy richness but now layer into it a wild-mushroom and warm-horse character of almost visceral appeal. In the mouth, Northern Rhône Syrah is often resoundingly fruity – and you have to call that fruit 'blackcurrants', as often as not. The difference from the no-less-blackcurranty Cabernet Sauvignon is one of register: Cabernet is a bass; Syrah a tenor. The Syrah blackcurrants weave and shuttle, soar and fall; in general, there is always a sense of vividness and purity, even ethereality, about its fruit, as if it had learned a trick or two from Pinot Noir a little further north still. Acidity is often prominent (and in poor vintages obtrusive) within it. But aroma, for me, is the key. If it's red, and it smells of flowers, it has to be young Syrah.

Everyone is in love with Syrah at present; no doubt it will be collecting Oscars in a year or two, and schoolgirls will stand screaming at it from behind temporary barriers. From its Northern Rhône fastness, it has been moving downriver and out across the South of France, chasing away Carignan as it does so, to great and beneficial effect. Syrah responds to carbonic maceration (see section 20) with redoubled aromatic enthusiasm. Now ambitious growers in Spain, Italy, California, Washington, Chile and Argentina are planting it, too, and the results can be as creamy, as sexy, as vigorous and as thigh-lickin' good as anything back home. I'm tempted, in the light of all this, to say that Syrah is the real Merlot. Bad Syrah, though, is a pretty uncomfortable experience: harsh, sour and splintery, whereas bad Merlot is usually just boring.

And then there's Shiraz: Syrah in Australia (and South Africa). It's the same grape, but it tends to taste very different from the Syrah that grows up overlooking the Rhône. Ordinary, hick versions in both countries can be coarse, rasping and rude, and there are many Australian formula wines made with Shiraz that are standard, tedious emulsions of added acid, added oak and simple, primitive fruit flavour. But great Aussie Shiraz is a depth-charging world original: black, with aromas and flavours which seem to have seeped up out of the old, burnt Australian land like a slow volcanic treacle. These wines smell leathery, jammy and port-like, and have thick and thunderous flavours of ripe blackberries, spice, salt, caramel and liquorice. Once drunk, never forgotten.

55 Garnacha/Grenache: the chocolate giant

This is a big one: the second most widely planted grape variety in the world. Second to Spain's tedious white Airén, moreover, therefore the most widely planted good grape in the world. It has two Mediterranean heartlands: the Southern Rhône valley and the South of France in general; and all over Spain (whence it originated – thus the Spanish name 'Garnacha' ought to take precedence internationally over the French 'Grenache' – though it doesn't). It's also widely grown in all of Australia's older established areas; ditto for California; and it flourishes, too, in Sardinia (where it's called Cannonau) and the south of Italy in general. What's it like?

Not very deep in colour (the Spaniards and the Australians often manage to make a darker wine from it than the French), but usually high in alcohol, and sometimes colossally so: a head-turning 14.5 per cent is perfectly achievable with lowish yields and a hot summer. Raisins and chocolate are the flavour keys to Grenache, with a smooth, supple and sometimes soupy texture; this is the sweetest and most comforting of dry red wines. Occasionally it rises up out of this toothsome beatitude to produce something rather beefier, burlier and spicier, especially in Australia, but it never has much finesse or poise. Simple Garnacha is jammy.

You might think, reading this, that it's the opposite of Syrah, and you wouldn't be far out: that's why they marry well together in blends. Syrah plays Jack Sprat, who'd eat no fat; Grenache is the voluminous Mrs Sprat, who disdained lean. They leave a nice clean platter behind them.

Oh, and one last thing: Garnacha makes damn fine rosé in France, Spain and Australia: deep red-pink or orange-pink, heady and round-contoured.

56 Sangiovese: coffee and passion

Imagine someone asked you to invent a new soft drink. You came up with an idea for a fizzy drink that was kind of brown in colour, right? – a sort of faecal brown in fact, without any noticeable fruit flavours. Instead, the flavours come from the same leaves which are used to produce cocaine, right, and some African nuts which contain caffeine, and some caramel. Hey! How far do you think you'd get?

The marketing men would take one look, brand you a fudge-brained dipstick, and you'd never be allowed to tout ideas in this town again. All the same, people seem to enjoy Coca-Cola.

That's more or less how I feel about Sangiovese. It makes red wines which break all the rules about what people should like – and people still like it. Indeed, in Chianti it has produced one of the world's best-known wine names and best-loved wine styles. Most pleasing. So much for marketing, which Burgundy winemaker Jean-Marie Guffens once told me was 'the art of selling rubbish to idiots'.

If you think back to section 39 and our division of the taste of wines into acids, tannins and richness, Sangiovese often seems to miss out almost entirely on the richness. It has lots of acid, and often lots of tannin, too; only when a serious grower and a good vintage come together does the richness pull into balance to give something round and resonant, though the ever-present acidity will ensure it also has a kind of tremulous quality, like a celebrated tenor giving the top note full vibrato. It smells of unusual things like coffee and stones and laurel leaves, though fruits can get a look in, too – and spices, when a little fresh oak comes into the equation. In the mouth, the key fruit in bad Chianti is apples, and in good Chianti plums; with time, the wine can tickle the coffee trigger again. The tannins are deliciously palpable, and sometimes bitter-edged. Above all, though (and this is very Italian), there is an energy there, a passion, a lunging or seizing quality, an edginess, sometimes an aggressiveness; no one ever said of a Sangiovese that it 'slips down nicely' or that it's 'soft and smooth'. Weak examples are horribly thin and acidulous.

Why has it had such success? Food, in a word: station yourself behind a mound of pasta, and try tackling it with the softest, smoothest red you can find. Boring! Then try the same experiment the next day with a decent Sangiovese and, suddenly, everything slips into place. That lively, lunging quality comes to the digestive-aiding rescue, and those coffeeish aromas and flavours provide welcome intrigue and distraction.

It has travelled, but without great success: like

Merlot, it seems to suffer from personality-loss abroad. Argentina has made the best go of it, but it tends to produce a wine more readily defined as Argentinian (tangy, sweet-and-sour) than as Sangiovese.

57
Nebbiolo: the prince in the mist

If you were to choose a variety to act as the hero in the romantic novel you're about to write, this is your grape. The high-born Nebbiolo is mysterious, dark and handsome. Shy too, though, and retiring, rarely leaving his mist-blanketed, castle-strewn, limestone-soiled North Italian fastness, a red grape who takes late ripening to nail-biting extremes, and who rewards the brave with dark, profound wines which unfold in bottle at the speed of coastal erosion. If you're nice to me, I might give you his phone number.

In statistical terms, Nebbiolo really doesn't deserve an entry to itself: there's 61 times as much Grenache planted in the world and 28 times as much Cabernet; you're unlikely to come across many bottles with this name on the label. Through Barolo and Barbaresco, though, it exerts a kind of authority over the drinking imagination, occupying one extreme of the red-grape spectrum. If you thought Cabernet could be severe and structured, just wait until you meet a young, craggy Nebbiolo. Tannin seems to drift through it like sunbeams through a midsummer forest, accompanied by fissuring acids and intense, extravagant extract. Its fruits (black cherries, black plums) are quiet and supportive, not overt, yet it has the capacity to be remarkably aromatic and allusive in other respects: tar and roses

are the classic triggers, but you may also find dried
and bitter herbs, liquorice, leather and tobacco
flavours in good Nebbiolo. Above all, it's strong –
and I'm not talking about alcohol. It's strongly
constructed, strongly constituted, strongly flavoured;
it's got the kind of jaw line which makes you reach
for a camera and backlighting. In time's theatre, too,
it has the strength to endure – provided that it was
ripe initially. Unripe or rain-diluted Nebbiolo is
spiky, sour and ungracious, the aristocracy at its
arrogant worst.

58 Tempranillo: getting along fine

If Nebbiolo is a desirable but moody bachelor, then
Tempranillo is a happily married man. It's been
deeply in love for as long as anyone can remember –
with oak, particularly American white oak, to the
extent that its own flavours are sometimes confused
with those of oak itself. (The same can be said of
Chardonnay.) Not only that, but it's so easy-going
and amenable that it loves to get involved in blends
with other grapes, and quickly subsumes its own
personality to that of the partnership. The net result
of all of this is that even wine drinkers with
thousands of bottle-miles under their belts remain a
little hazy about exactly how Tempranillo tastes.

For all that, it's Spain's greatest grape, the one
which takes the lead role in Rioja and occupies the
whole stage in Ribera del Duero. In other regions,
too, it's often the red grape of choice, though it may
be called Tinto Fino, Cencibel or Ull de Llebre. Give
it the gun, as they do most whole-heartedly in Ribera
del Duero, and it can produce a dark, rumply,
chocolate-and-plum-flavoured red with lots of soft

tannins and juicy balancing acids: classic in every way, and sometimes excitingly dense. Elsewhere, particularly after it's swooned into the arms of a white-oak cask for a few years and got intimately involved with Garnacha, it is a much paler and softer red, beaming beneficently as it hands around bowls of strawberries and leaves a trail of vanilla in the air. Mix it with Cabernet, and it seems to climb into the back seat, though its general willingness to fill out flavour, to fetch and carry, to support and soothe, means that such blends are much more smiley affairs than Cabernet on its own would be.

As yet, it hasn't travelled widely, but it will. It plays a role in port as Tinta Roriz, and it's also widely planted in Argentina (where it's called Tempranilla). As with Sangiovese, though, the results are more Argentinian than varietal: it's just another light, rounded, bitter-sweet red there.

59
Chardonnay: all things to all palates

Here's a grape success story. Thirty years ago, most wine drinkers would have been mystified as to what Chardonnay was – though they would have been familiar enough with Chablis and other white burgundies, all of them made from Chardonnay alone.

Today, Chardonnay has become the one wine name which every drinker knows. Many drinkers, indeed, don't even realise it's a grape, but consider it a brand in its own right. The latest big hit on British wine-shop shelves is Sparkling Chardonnay (which must make the stiff-backed producers of Blanc de Blancs Champagne, also a sparkling Chardonnay, grimace wryly). Never mind that, in the warm climates from which these wines come, Chardonnay isn't necessarily the best grape for sparkling wines; the point is that people feel happy with the name.

I've seen shirts called Chardonnay, and heard of pets called Chardonnay, and slept in hotel rooms and even entire hotels named after Chardonnay; before long, someone is bound to produce a car called a Chardonnay, and then there'll be a weepy movie about a cute girl called Chardonnay involved in an unhappy love affair with a handsome older man (who probably won't be called Cabernet), and Eurovision Song Contest entries from a band called Chardonnay, and maybe even a tv soap set in a fictitious Australian wine-growing community called Chardonnay. As it happens, there is a village called Chardonnay in France's Mâcon region. If only they spoke English ...

And it's just a grape. A nice one: easy to grow in all sorts of places, good yields, lots of sugar, simple to vinify, attractive flavours. All the little white grapes want to be Chardonnay when they grow up.

The basic fruit flavour of Chardonnay is often likened to lemons (of a soft and gentle sort), but its success with wine consumers at large is due to the fact that it is able to take on all sorts of other flavours. In fruit terms, it can also suggest apples, limes, oranges and, especially in sunny climates, summer fruits like peach, apricot and melon, and occasionally tropical fruits such as mango. Aromatically, you can find all these fruits playing a role, as well as fugitive flower and blossom aromas, such as acacia, honeysuckle and hawthorn. "Big mouthfeel and viscosity" is Australian winemaker Brian Croser's explanation of another of Chardonnay's assets: its comforting texture as it crosses the tongue.

Increasingly nowadays, promising Chardonnays

are fermented in new oak barrels; after fermentation is finished, too, the wine continues to age in the barrels, with the lees being stirred up into it at regular intervals. This gives the wine a marked milkiness or creaminess, as well as integrating the richly vanillic, toasty flavour of the oak itself softly and harmoniously. (You can get the milkiness without the toast by ageing Chardonnay on its lees in stainless-steel tanks.)

As Chardonnay ages, it can turn buttery at first, and later richly nutty. This is even true of Chardonnay which has never been anywhere near an oak barrel. Indeed the reason why richly oaky Chardonnay from warm climates such as California's Napa valley or Australia's Barossa valley has been such an extravagant success with consumers is that it duplicates, in three years, what the finest white burgundy can only achieve in ten or fifteen. Not always as subtly, of course, but if a bottle invites your tongue to a sauna, climbs all over it, rubs creams into it, and generally gives it a very good time, who's complaining?

Chardonnay, as I said, began life in Burgundy, where it produces everything from the steeliest, sharpest, greenest and slenderest of Chablis down to the softly honeyed, comforting whites of Mâcon and its 'Villages'. Between the two come the greatest Chardonnays in the world, those of central Burgundy: the Montrachets and Corton-Charlemagnes, which legendarily make pompous and self-important men remove their hats and fall to their knees. Of all the wines I know, none need age more than these. Drink them young and they're positively boring: hard, inarticulate, morose. Give them ten or twenty years' age and they turn orchestral, rich and arm-wavingly expansive. It's difficult to believe, indeed, that any white wine can contain so much aroma and wealth of flavour. These are the wines that inspire the world's Chardonnay-growers; these are the wines that have made this grape the most widely travelled in history.

Let's not overlook Champagne, though. Chardonnay is the only white grape used there, and if you ever get the chance to taste the base Chardonnay used in Champagne blends, you won't believe your taste buds. It seems like pure lemon juice, so sharp and sour is it. How can this ugly duckling ever turn into a swanlike glass of Champagne? Age and yeast, Chardonnay's old allies, provide the answer.

Everyone everywhere is trying to make great Chardonnay, and it's another testament to the amenability and versatility of this grape that none of these efforts can be dismissed outright. California has probably had greater success than anywhere else – and is there a sexier wine in the world than one of California's unctuous, heady, high-sheen, silk-stocking Chards? Yet Australia (all of it, from the hot Hunter and Barossa valleys and warm Margaret River to cool Yarra and chilly Tasmania), New Zealand, South Africa, Argentina and Chile have made Chardonnays which demand and reward thoughtful drinking; within Europe, Spain, Italy, Greece and even Austria can produce complex, finely crafted Chardonnays, too, though exactly what style these are made in depends on the ambitions and tastes of the winemaker.

In the end, that's Chardonnay's great draw: it rewards human intervention more than most grapes, and in doing so provides lots of enjoyment for drinkers.

60

Riesling: the tightrope walker

Riesling is Chardonnay's opposite. If Chardonnay is a blonde, Riesling has black hair. If Chardonnay is worldly and easy-going, flicking through the fashion pages of magazines with a packet of cigarettes on one side and a tub of ice cream on the other, Riesling is up in her bedroom studying Buddhism and listening to Brahms. If Chardonnay is neon, big city lights, and sleek cars out on the freeway, Riesling is a candle flickering behind the leaded window of a half-timbered house, beneath a protective lime tree in a quiet village.

In aroma and flavour, the two grapes have a greatly contrasting outlook on the world; they set off through time, too, in different directions. Chardonnay leaves its gentle fruits behind it as early as possible, to get languidly lost in a world of cream, butter and nuts; whereas Riesling is utterly committed to maintaining its remarkable spectrum of fresh fruit flavours throughout what is often a long life. The only non-fruit note it regularly acquires is a strangely appealing whiff of petrol or kerosene.

The two grapes fail to agree, too, over barrels. Chardonnay loves oak, meshing and melding its own flavours with those surrendered by the wood; Riesling hates it, since its flavours become confused and muddled and lose impact after a spell in cask.

But, above all, it's the balance within each wine that is different: Champagne and some Chablis aside, Chardonnay is a spreading, settling, broad-beamed, plump and comely wine with palpable structure and vinosity. Riesling, especially in its German homeland, is a tightrope-walking wine, perpetually teetering between the gravitational pulls of acidity on one side and sweetness on the other, with the structural safety net of vinosity and alcohol almost completely absent. This particular act can be one of thrilling beauty –

though if your mouth has grown accustomed to the busty width and brawny dimensions of Chardonnay and other white wines of 12 or 13 per cent alcohol, enjoying a ballerina-like German Riesling of just eight or nine per cent to the full requires a conscious effort of adjustment. (If you can't adjust, try Australian Rieslings which have 12 or 13 per cent alcohol.)

It is this inherent balance which gives Riesling its versatility. Not, Chardonnay-like, in the variety of vinification treatments and approaches it can be given, but in the fact that Riesling can make wines of every level of sweetness, from fully dry to sugar-saturated, without ever losing its edge and definition. Few grapes respond better to the beneficent depredations of botrytis, either, than Riesling; the mould adds further layers of complexity to what is already a many-tiered flavour.

German Rieslings are an inspiring extreme. Elsewhere in the world, under warmer skies, the balance achieved by Riesling grows more conventional, and a core of alcohol gives the fruit flavours something to wrap themselves around. The fruit spectrum changes, too, from crisp, edgy, electrical jolts of apple and peach, grape and grapefruit, apricot and tangerine towards rounder, swimmier spoonfuls of mango, pineapple, lychee and papaya. In Australia's celebrated Riesling-growing areas (the Clare and Eden valleys), lime is the archetypal taste, backed up by some of the oily astringency of citrus pith and peel in general. But fruit is always the key to Riesling; it is this light-footed, dancing, exuberant and sometimes heart-wrenching fruitiness that gives it such a vivid personality, and makes it, as the future will prove, every bit as great a grape as Chardonnay. Its problem is being taken seriously enough in the first place – by growers, in order to get good vineyard land and low

crop levels, and by consumers, in order to reward
those growers who have given it the respect it
deserves.

61
Sauvignon Blanc: the Big Green

Most wines, when they're young at any rate, taste of
fruit – and Sauvignon Blanc is no exception to this
rule. Apples, citrus fruits and gooseberries are just
three of the fruit triggers that wine made from this
vigorous white variety might suggest. What makes it
unique, though, is not its fruit hints, but another side
of its character altogether. The sixteenth-century
English poet Andrew Marvell probably never tasted
it, but summed it up perfectly in his poem 'The
Garden'.

... Annihilating all that's made
To a green Thought in a green Shade.

Among grape varieties, Sauvignon Blanc is the only
one capable of suggesting, with vivid exactitude,
vegetation in all its moods, from a sweet-scented,
low-flying overview of fine snipped fronds to the
insect-chomping smack of sap and the ooze of
chlorophyll. Nearly all Sauvignon Blanc wines have a
generalised leafiness ('blackcurrant buds' is the very
precise French term), and some take this to
extremes, throwing up a great hum of herbaceous
aroma as an English lawn might in June, after an
afternoon of ferocious mowing. If you've ever slashed
your way through a bed of nettles or trimmed a
hedge, too, you'll be familiar with the Sauvignon
repertoire. The compounds responsible for these
aromas are called methoxypyrazines, and are actively
solicited by some producers of this variety through

the use of shaded canopies and special yeasts.

Not only does Sauvignon Blanc suggest vegetal aromas and flavours, but it also suggests out-and-out vegetable triggers, too. Sometimes, gentle ones like fennel or celery, but more often overt ones like asparagus, for example, or tinned peas. Unsuccessful Sauvignon can sometimes resemble decomposing mushrooms.

Nor is that all. In its French stronghold, in the central and upper Loire valley, Sauvignon also acquires a distinctive, smoky, mineral quality, customarily called 'flinty' (suggestive both of flintstones and pebbles in themselves, but also of the traditional fire-raising role of flints as, for example, in a flintlock gun mechanism). There is a feral side of its personality, too, an obscure degeneration of both smokiness and herbaceousness: cat's pee. I won't rub your nose in it.

Most of the Sauvignon we have been describing so far is unoaked. Because the variety has an intrinsically vivacious personality (born of its relatively high acid levels), it does not necessarily need or respond well to oak. Most of the wines in the most famous Sauvignon-growing areas, which are certainly France's Upper Loire (Sancerre and Pouilly-Fumé) and New Zealand (especially pebbley Marlborough), go to market unoaked.

Yet, where Sauvignon is grown in a slightly warmer climate, or where it is blended with other grape varieties, the more ambitious examples may be given oak, often to sumptuous effect. The famous blends of Sauvignon Blanc with Sémillon in Bordeaux's Graves and Pessac-Léognan can achieve a magnificently light-fingered richness: the texture of damask; the aromas and flavours of vegetable sauces and reductions given an urbane, lemony lift.

Sounds good, doesn't it? And Sauvignon Blanc is, indeed, a popular wine, both from the areas I've mentioned and from others, too, like South Africa (especially its cool, coastal vineyards at Constantia and elsewhere) and Australia (Adelaide Hills and Coonawarra). There are, though, three minor qualifications to make before we pull the shutter down on this happy picture.

The first is that Sauvignon's popularity means that it is planted in a lot of areas to which it is ill suited, and from which over-large crops are taken: such Sauvignons vary from the thoroughly boring (a vaguely leafy white) to the actively unpleasant (either sharp, thin and sour or sickly sweet). The second qualification is that some 'Sauvignon Blanc' is in fact Sauvignon Vert or Sauvignonasse, a shallower and more trivial variety; this is a particular problem in Chile. The third qualification is that, for all the fun and enjoyment of this 'personality' of the wine world, it can be a mite monotonous, a one-glass wine. On that, though, the decision's yours.

62 Chenin Blanc: the wastrel genius

If someone was to offer me a two-week holiday with a particular grape variety, I think I'd choose Chenin Blanc.

Back in its university days, Chenin was the student who stayed apart from the others, who disappeared from time to time, who kept an air of mystery wrapped about him or her like a cloak. There was huge talent there, everyone knew, but also a contrary spirit which meant that the promise didn't always emerge, and was sometimes thrown away completely, almost on a whim. Chenin, we all knew, could make a great success of its life, or it could all end in waste and disaster.

The jury's still out; the mystery remains. That's

why I'd like to spend that time with Chenin – to find out exactly why some of its wines are so sensationally good, and others downright ugly and offensive, and to find out, too, exactly which of the three or four stylistic faces it offers to the world is the real Chenin.

The two countries where Chenin is taken most seriously (though it is grown to a limited extent in others, too) are France and South Africa. In France, it is the grape of choice in the Central Loire valley – for appellations such as Vouvray, Anjou, Saumur, Savennières, Quarts de Chaume and Bonnezeaux – and as the grape providing most of the base wine for the sparkling wines made in the Loire valley, too. We have in our sights, here, wines of great coarseness and crudity, and some of the most intensely beautiful white wines in the world, both dry and sweet. The word 'mercurial' might have been invented for Loire Chenin Blanc.

Flavours, though; you want flavours. Dry Chenin Blanc from the Loire valley varies from piercingly dry, limey and sharp (in appellations such as Jasnières), like Sauvignon Blanc without the distraction of its vegetal notes, to (in Savennières) a remarkably broad-backed, rich and bready wine, linden-scented, the sort of thing which, after a ripe year, could be confused with top-flight white burgundy. In between lie all sorts of strangenesses, often intense in flavour but often, too, raw and harsh, reminding the drinker of nothing so much as chopped apple cores. When it's good, wax and honey play about a pure and elegant grape-and-greengage fruit. What Chenin always has, though, is a sort of strength, power or mastery of flavour, a driving and penetrating quality, which gives its best wines magnificence and its worst active ugliness.

In terms of sweetness, too, Chenin offers a puzzling continuum. Much Chenin is dry; much is not. Some appellations (such as the well known

Vouvray) are for dry, medium-sweet and sweet white wines, while others (such as Quarts de Chaume and Bonnezeaux) for sweet wines alone; there are even special local terms, like *moelleux* (which literally means 'marrowy') for sweetish or sweet wines. In the Loire valley, sweet Chenin begins life with a range of pretty, crystallised fruit flavours and slowly, over the years, amplifies these fruit flavours into a deep, limpid profundity.

For Loire-valley Chenin, age counts. The best wines, both dry and sweet, need age in order to learn manners, to lose the harsh violence and abruptness of their youth, and to order their flavours more agreeably and harmoniously. Not only that, but the most beautiful elements of Chenin's flavour, the eloquent, oboe-like descants it can make on themes of honey and beeswax, of damp straw and white pepper, only emerge after a few years in bottle. The very best can age a lifetime. When fully mature, at 20 or 25 years, a glass of sweet Chenin gives you the impression that you're dipping your nose into a deep, mossy well only to find, with Alice-like wonder, that the well is filled with the perfectly preserved juices of orchard fruits mingled with the purest honey.

Sparkling wines based on Chenin are in some ways off to a bad start. Traditional practice in the Loire has meant that sparkling wine is what you use your Chenin for if it hasn't ripened successfully, or if there's been a bad vintage. There often seems to be a hardness and an unyielding quality to all but the best.

We could spend six months in the Loire, drinking Chenin every day; then someone could slide a glass of South African Chenin under our noses and neither of us would even be able to recognise it as the same grape. In South Africa (where it was traditionally called Steen), it makes a much more conventionally fruity wine, often characterised by guava and passion-fruit notes. The problem is that it has been South Africa's workhorse grape, the one no one took too seriously, so it hasn't been given the prime vineyard land nor the fancy winery treatment. This is beginning to change now, as visiting winemakers have noticed the impressive age of some of the Chenin vines. Fruit from these older vines is being barrel-fermented (something no Loire-valley Frenchman would ever do) to provide a worthwhile alternative to yet more barrel-fermented Chardonnay, giving less dairy-maid richness and more vanillic complexity to what remains relatively fresh and peppery fruit.

63 Sémillon: something to chew on

The French novelist and short-story writer Guy de Maupassant wrote a tale called *Boule de Suif*, a title generally translated into English as 'Suet Dumpling'. *Boule de Suif* was the nickname of a plump prostitute who found herself, in time of war, sharing a long carriage journey with a handful of 'respectable' folk, all of whom disdained her company and kept themselves aloof from her scandalous person. Snowy conditions mean the journey drags on, and on, and on; no one has brought any food or drink with them. No one, that is, apart from Boule de Suif herself, who gets out a carefully prepared picnic basket full of tasty morsels: two chickens carved up and embedded in aspic; lark pâté; a slab of Pont-l'Évêque cheese; bottles of claret. She offers to share her picnic with the others – who gradually (men first) lose their scruples about her company, and eventually tuck in with avid relish and opportune friendliness. At the long journey's end, of course, after further and darker adventures, they spurn her again, refusing to repay her kindness and resuming a surly censure of what she represents.

Boule de Suif, it seems to me, would be an excellent nickname for the Sémillon grape. It looks very round and yellow on the vine, and it makes very plump, friendly and comforting white wines. Indeed, in the Sauternes region of Bordeaux, which is where it began life, it makes some of the fattest, most opulent sweet wines in the world. These unctuous wines seem to glisten and sweat sweetness, just as buns and cakes made with lard seem to glisten and sweat as they beckon the hungry from shop windows.

Physically, Sémillon is relatively thin-skinned, which means that it is deliciously vulnerable to attack by botrytis spores. It also surrenders itself with exceptional pleasure to the embrace of oak – and oak provides an important element of the richness of flavour you'll find in good Sauternes. Oak, too, plays a major role in most dry Sémillon wines, both in Bordeaux and elsewhere.

Sémillon in Bordeaux is usually used in a blend with Sauvignon Blanc, though Sémillon is often the dominant partner. In Graves and Pessac-Léognan, this duo provides dry white wines that furnish the drinker with a creaminess altogether different from Chardonnay's; here it is discreet, urbane and nuanced, studded with both soft fruit and vegetal notes, as a chicken might be studded with garlic or truffles.

Away from Bordeaux, it is Australia which has chiefly made a go of Sémillon (where it loses its 'é'). It remains, though, a friendly, lardy kind of grape which takes well to oak, and has the added virtue of acquiring a distinctive Australian character to its fruit. (This makes it, you could say, the white Shiraz.) In fruit terms, French Sémillon is relatively discreet; Australian Semillon, by contrast, fairly hums with aromas variously assigned to lime pith, toast, custard, broad beans, dry straw and even cheese. In flavour these notes receive a softer echo, with lime pith generally to the fore. A big contrast to Chardonnay, in other words; and while Aussie Chardonnay ages unpredictably, sometimes taking on extra depths but just as often falling entirely to pieces and tasting like cardboard, Semillon generally ages well, honing and refining that distinctive, faintly abrasive character it has. It reminds me, aurally, of a goose honking. "I'm here," it seems to say; "I exist; let's have fun."

Inspired (as ever) by Bordeaux, most wine-producing countries have begun work on Semillon, but I find the results often mealy, mushy and disappointing. The Australian experience, though, suggests that the vine is relatively adaptable, so things may change. Keep your palates peeled.

64 Pinot Gris: a whiff of smoke

The seductive and exasperating Pinot Noir, which we met back in section 51, has a couple of white cousins or, to be more gothically accurate, mutations: Pinot Gris (grey Pinot) and Pinot Blanc (white Pinot). You'll find a short profile of Pinot Blanc in the grape-variety round-up constituted by section 66; in my tasting notebook, though, Pinot Gris is altogether the more interesting grape. Since it's beginning to do a little more travelling than it used to, I thought we might all spend a paragraph or two together.

Burgundy (where it's called Pinot Beurot) is its home, but Alsace is where it has most, so far, to say for itself. Indeed, in some ways it seems to be the grape variety that most accurately sums up the wine-drinking ideals of that hungry, sunny patch of northern-eastern France, since it is, above all, a plump and roundly fruity white. Doughboy-plump; orchard-fruity. The thrill in Pinot Gris comes when a skilled winegrower and a good patch of earth combine to give those fruity characters (grape, apple and nectarine) an oily and succulent density, as if they had been bubbled down into a Danish pastry. Sometimes the wine stops there, fixing on that sweetly fruity density. Sometimes, though, as it sits on the tongue as firmly as a sow on straw, it seems also to surrender an alluringly smoky quality. I don't mean the combative flintlock strike of a Sauvignon Blanc, but something more akin to frying bacon or a simmering ham hock. Very greedy and gluttonous, it is. Pass me that napkin; my lips need a wipe.

Pinot Gris is sometimes called Tokay d'Alsace, for no very good reason; in Italy it's called Pinot Grigio. It's one of northern Italy's more important and more popular whites, though all too often it lacks any of the pork-belly richness and generosity that the best French examples have, and is more slender and green in style.

The other place in which it has proved popular so far is Oregon. Depending on the ambitions of the producer there, it either provides a good unoaked alternative to Chardonnay or quite simply takes over as 'prime white' where Chardonnay left off. Typical Oregonian Pinot Gris captures the slightly misty, autumnal, jam-simmering feel of that state's wines, with rounded pear or greengage notes. As yet, though, any smoky character will be founded on the toasted barrels that Oregon Pinot Gris may be aged in, rather than on the oily density of its fruit.

Look out, too, for inexpensive, cherub-fruited and occasionally musky examples from Hungary (where it is sometimes known by the local name Szürkebarát), and rather more expensive and refined efforts from Germany and Austria (where it may be called Grauburgunder when dry and Ruländer when sweetish). What you'll notice about the latter is that they lack the vivid, crystalline impact and balance of Riesling; instead, they communicate a softness and fullness of fruit with some of the sponge-cake or yeast-dough richness I alluded to earlier.

65
Viognier: come up and see me some time

What? You want to know what the most extravagant wine aroma I've ever come across smelled like? Fair enough. Normally the 'best ever' questions are difficult to answer (because, professor, all reality is experienced subjectively), but in this case I can give you a straight reply.

The smell of this pale yellow, noticeably glycerous yet dry white wine came charging out of the glass like a cat out of a cold bath. Flowers, so far as I remember, were the first thing I thought of – not just a generalised florality, but all sorts of specific flowers. There was the fresh delicacy of freesias, for example, and the washday fragrance of jasmine; I thought I caught a little sweet honeysuckle in there, too, and something of the musky heaviness of lilies and gardenias. There were other aromas, too, which reminded me of fine cosmetics: supple creams and lotions whose boxes might carry addresses in Paris's 16th arrondissement. There was also something indefinably sexy about the wine's scent – the smell, let's say, of the taut skin of a good-looking twenty-three-year-old who's just stepped out of the shower. Strangely enough, there were barely any fruit notes there to speak of: a slice of apricot, possibly, sprinkled with a little peach juice. And white pepper: where did that come from? For all their intensity, the scents were well ordered and composed; there was none of the oppressiveness of cut-price perfume about them. I sniffed, repeatedly. Was this really wine?

It was. It was Yves Cuilleron's 1994 Condrieu les Chaillets Vieilles Vignes. Expensive, for such a young, unoaked wine: around four times the price of a decent Chilean Chardonnay. Yet one whiff told the drinker he or she had bought wisely. There just isn't much on this earth to eat or drink which smells so good.

Enter, to thunderous applause, the Viognier grape variety. It's no surprise, given that it can perform that kind of act, that it's being planted in vineyards all around the temperate world as you read this. Viognier steps forward, blinks shyly; it's really not used to all this limelight. Twenty years ago, people were discussing its imminent extinction. Condrieu is a tiny little morsel of the northern Rhône valley, and growers could barely be bothered with this tiresome, irregularly flowering, poorly fruiting variety any more.

Fortunately, a few growers, such as the affable Georges Vernay, persisted. The result is that Viognier lived on to tell its aromatic tale (in the mouth, it tastes roughly like it smells, though the base of softly spicy, low acid, apricot fruit plays more of an active role), inspiring the present wave of plantings and graftings.

Before you rush out, expecting the first cheap varietal Viognier you can lay your hands on to enchant and seduce, a word of warning. Viognier from the Condrieu fastness is a wine produced from often tiny yields. The Viognier on offer from the Languedoc, Chile or Australia at a quarter of its price may be produced at four times the yield – and its character slips away under these circumstances like memory with age. You'll be getting a vaguely aromatic, plumpish dry white, full stop. The one place where Viognier has so far been taken with extreme seriousness so far is California, and the results there can be excitingly rich and heady. At a price, alas, more or less indistinguishable from Condrieu's own.

66
Other grape variety profiles

There are thousands of grape varieties. I have tried to include, in this section, those which you may encounter as varietal wines rather than those customarily used as blending varieties.

Aglianico (red)
Grand and gutsy southern Italian red, with complex, bitter-edged, dark chocolate flavours.

Airén (white)
Dull, dead-loss white – and also (thanks to the fact that it sprawls across the heart of Spain) the world's most widely planted grape variety. Much is, sensibly, burnt for brandy.

Albariño (white)
Delicate, peachy white from Spain's Galicia and (as Alvarinho) Portugal's Vinho Verde country.

Alicante Bouschet (red)
One of the very few red grapes with red juice, producing ink-black, rough-edged, rumpy-pumpy wines.

Aligoté (white)
Sharpish white from Burgundy: I prefer it with crème de cassis, as a kir.

Aramon (red)
Horrible old red variety, formerly used to produce industrial wine in France's Midi. On the way out, praise be.

Arneis (white)
Piedmontese white variety meant to resemble

almonds; it always seems dull to me.

Bacchus (white)

Musky, sometimes pretty wines from this grape are made in Germany and England.

Barbera (red)

Impressive variety of northern Italy – after a good summer. Its late-ripening habits, though, mean that at all times it has high acidity levels, not always balanced (as they should be) by pungent raspberry fruit. Can stab like a fencer; take care.

Blaufränkisch (red)

Vivid, lively red from Austria, known as Limberger or Lemberger in Germany and elsewhere, and Kékfrankos in Hungary.

Bonarda (red)

Soft, juicy wine from this variety is widely grown in Argentina.

Carignan (red)

Carignan once spread across southern France and north Africa like sunlight, and indeed much is still planted there – as well as in Spain, too, as Cariñena. It's one of those varieties which has almost swung back into fashion recently, as producers saw how old the vines were, and worked out that 'Old-vine Carignan' might have an appealingly traditional ring to it. It's also much used as a blending component, to 'add acidity', they say. I hate it: it tastes like aspirins to me, harsh and raw, and pollutes otherwise good wines.

Chasselas (white)

Widely planted grape which can be eaten as fruit or made into wine. It reaches its soft and buttery peak in Switzerland (where it's also known as Fendant).

Cinsault (red)

Cinsault can be a bit like Grenache: toffeed and sweet. Made carefully, it can also have freshness and perfume. What it never has much of is colour or tannin; it's not a gutsy red.

Colombard (white)
Simple, light, pleasant and fruity.
Dolcetto (red)
The name means 'the little sweet one' in Italian and, relative to other Piedmont reds, I guess it might be seen in that way; deep colours, too. But in the universal scheme of things it's still very Piedmontese: pungent, challenging, cutting and lively, with vigorous plum fruit.
Dornfelder (red)
German crossing: dark and boisterous.
Fernão Pires (white)
Intriguing lazy, heavy-lidded Portuguese white, also known as Maria Gomes.
Feteasca (white)
Musky, plump East-European speciality.
Freisa (red)
Strange, light, raspberryish Piedmontese red.
Furmint (white)
Aristocratic, reserved yet complex Hungarian variety, with both high acidity and rich substance.
Gamay (red)
Red-wine grape used for Beaujolais, generally producing bright, aromatic wines that have flavours of cherry and raspberry but the texture of white wine. Only occasionally does it achieve any sort of chewiness or textural depth.
Gewürztraminer (white)
A white wine from pink berries, this, and singular in other ways, too. If it's perfume that you're after, then a good and typical Gewürztraminer is out there at the aromatic limits with Viognier. Spice and flowers are its two main aromatic suggestibles; other scent triggers may include rose-water, lychees and cold cream. In the mouth, these notes continue to bombard your olfactory bulb, backed up by often generous alcohol but reticent fruit, giving a rather galumphing, four-square character to the wine. Less

successful examples (most of those produced outside Alsace) are often mawkish and sweet, lacking aromatic power. Traminer is a cousin of similar style.

Grüner Veltliner (white)

Austria's pleasant, though generally neutral, workhorse: try looking for a little pepper.

Hárslevelü (white)

Softish, aromatic Hungarian variety, used to get Furmint to relax a little. Pretty linden style (the name means 'lime leaf').

Irsai Oliver (white)

Hungarian cross producing attractive if simple, aromatic, Muscat-like wines.

Kadarka (red)

Generally lightish in its native Hungary and (as Gamza) softish in Bulgaria.

Kerner (white)

Widely planted German Riesling-Trollinger cross: pleasant but low personality.

Lagrein (red)

Grape used for quenching reds and rosés in the Italian Alps.

Lambrusco (red)

A variety as well as a wine. The best is dry, frothy and bitter-edged.

Laski Rizling (white)

Lively, sometimes crisp white, but not The Real Thing. Also known as Welschriesling.

Malbec (red)

Moderately common grape variety often used in blends; on its own (most notably in Argentina), it produces reds with lots of stuffing and savoury qualities but sometimes restrained fruit. Also known as Côt, Auxerrois and by various alternative spellings of Malbec.

Malvasia (white and red)

Big family of varieties. Usually blended; rather soft and soapy on its own.

Manseng (white)
Two white varieties (Gros and Petit) used in south-western France to produce sometimes fine, piquant whites and well balanced, late-harvest wines.

Marsanne (white)
One of two key Rhône valley white varieties, along with Roussanne; also grown in Australia. Marsanne is fat, glycerous and honeysuckle-scented, with rich, mallowy flavours (mango in Australia).

Mondeuse (red)
Deep, mineral-like wine from Savoie.

Montepulciano (red)
Central Italian variety providing juicy, plummy, well structured reds.

Morio-Muskat (white)
Grapy and appealing, if simple.

Mourvèdre (red)
Important variety in the south of France and (as Monastrell) in Spain; sometimes known as Mataro in the New World. Gutsy, well structured, often alcoholic wines with black olive and dark chocolate flavours and (sometimes though not always) blackberry fruit.

Müller-Thurgau (white)
High yielding and adaptable, but the wines from this vine aren't generally very good – save in English vineyards, when they can be fragrant and intense.

Muscadelle (white)
Dullish variety in most cases, though it can make fine 'Liqueur Tokay' in Australia.

Muscadet
A bit of a cheat, this, since the grape variety which makes Muscadet is in fact called Melon de Bourgogne. It's damn near neutral, providing a crisp, faintly lemony, super-dry white; this neutrality means that the best Muscadets are described as *sur lie* – ('on lees'), meaning that they are bottled straight off their yeast lees in order to give the wine both

maximum freshness and a little bready depth. That's the theory, anyway; sometimes it works.

Muscat (usually white)

Not so much a grape variety, but more an entire clan: some members produce table grapes, some mediocre wines, some fine wines (and the grapes can be white, yellow, brown, pink or red). In general, it's the easiest grape of all for wine tasters to recognize, and one that pleases wine-description conservatives, since it smells and tastes of ... grapes. It can be made as a dry wine, but is more often made into a sweet wine by fortification, since that throws its fragrance into the foreground, allowing it to saturate the sugars and alcohol in the wine, like a dye saturating cloth. Dry Muscat (usually labelled as such, save in Alsace) often smells pretty and grapy-fresh, but its flavour can lack middle-palate interest and fruity acid balance. Known as Tamîioasa in Romania.

Négrette (red)

Perfumed, light and peppery red from south-western France.

Negroamaro (red)

One of the finest grapes from southern Italy, Negroamaro produces wines with some of the raisin-and-chocolate notes of Grenache, thrown into a fine drinking balance by relatively lively acidity.

Nero d'Avola (red)

Sicily's great red variety, also known as Calabrese, capable of producing deep, rich reds which take well to ageing in oak or the local chestnut wood.

Parellada (white)

Apple-like white from Catalonia, used in Cava blends.

Pedro Ximénez (white)

When you see this name on a bottle, expect a supersweet wine with the colour and texture of treacle.

Petite Sirah (red)

Mysterious grape variety found in California, which produces very deep, black and rather clod-hopping wines.

Petit Verdot (red)

A minor Bordeaux grape, now causing ripples elsewhere. Its wine tends to be tannic, peppery and spicy.

Picpoul (white)

A grape variety remarkable chiefly for keeping its acidity under the Southern French sun. No great thrills.

Pinotage (red)

South Africa's speciality, this crossing of Cinsault and Pinot Noir can produce wines of greater depth and chewiness than either parent, with flavours of plum, prune and smoke; sometimes rubbery.

Pinot Blanc (white)

Simple fresh, grapy fruit, sometimes with vanillic overtones (even without oak). Also known as Weissburgünder and Pinot Bianco.

Plavac Mali (red)

Good solid stuff from Dalmatia. May be identical to Zinfandel.

Portugieser (red)

All-purpose red from Germany and Austria.

Prosecco (white)

Softly seedy white used for sparkling wines in northern Italy.

Refosco (red)

Another sharpish North Italian.

Rkatsiteli (white)

There are huge plantings all over the former Soviet Union of this perky, chunky white.

Roussanne (white)

The other white grape variety of France's Rhône valley; also known as Bergeron in Savoie. Roussanne is lighter and finer grained than Marsanne, with delicate scents of white hedgerow flowers like

hawthorn and cow parsley and subtle peach/apricot
fruit. One to watch.

Roussette (white)
Fresh, quicksilver wines from Savoie's mountains
(also known as Altesse).

St Laurent (red)
Perfumed, soft-textured Austrian red.

Scheurebe (white)
Weird but convincing German variety, producing
wines which variously suggest rose petals, walnuts,
grapefruit, blackcurrant, and, occasionally, something
feral, too.

Schönburger (white)
Yet another German crossing, chiefly useful for the
well balanced wine it can produce in Britain.

Seyval Blanc (white)
A hybrid, producing chunky, dry whites in difficult
climates like England's.

Silvaner (white)
Simple, clean, fresh wines from this variety grown in
Germany and Alsace (Sylvaner), with a faintly earthy
character.

Tannat (red)
Toughie found in south-western France: the Madiran
grape.

Tarrango (red)
Easy-going, confectionery-style, Australian crossing.

Teroldego Rotaliano (red)
Rough-edged, vivid red from Trentino in north Italy.

Tinta Barroca (red)
Port grape that also makes well rounded reds in
South Africa.

Tocai/Tocai Friuliano (white)
Nothing to do with Hungarian Tokaji (which is
Furmint and Hárslevelü) nor with Tokay d'Alsace
(which is Pinot Gris), this is in fact probably the
same as Sauvignonasse or Sauvignon Vert – which
the Chileans tend to label Sauvignon Blanc. Wouldn't

you love to be an ampelographer?* In drinking terms, Tocai is typically Italian – pleasant, crisp, relatively neutral.

Torrontés (white)

An Argentine speciality, wines from this grape variety usually resemble dry Muscat.

Touriga Nacional (red)

Perhaps the greatest of all port varieties, now increasingly used for table wines of dusty depth and tannic concentration.

Trebbiano (white)

In principle, low on character, but can have some fresh-fruit style if carefully vinified. Also known as Ugni Blanc.

Trollinger (red)

Exceptionally dull light red, common in southern Germany and (as Schiava) in northern Italy; it's also sold as the table grape Black Hamburg.

Verdelho (white)

Makes an off-dry Madeira of apple-sherbet character on its island home. When transplanted to Australia, Verdelho produces a juicy, lively white wine, with plenty of tropical-fruit notes.

Verdicchio (white)

Better than the Italian average, with a genuinely lemony quiver to it.

Vermentino (white)

Grown widely around the Mediterranean (it's also called Rolle), wines from this variety have a gently vegetal and aniseed character.

Vranac (red)

Grown in Montenegro, this variety makes the gutsiest and most impressive of the wines of the former Yugoslavia.

Zinfandel (red)

America's great 'native' grape (though in fact it's the Primitivo of southern Italy). Makes everything from basic reds of crashing simplicity (and, as 'Blush',

*botanist specialising in vines

sickly rosés) to deep, finely crafted wines of great fruit intensity and profundity. Opinions are divided as to whether Zinfandel wines age well.

Zweigelt (red)
Popular Austrian crossing, producing dark, vivid wines.

67 You can taste regions

When we set off on our mission, at the beginning of Part Five, to cut a path through the dense and chaotic undergrowth of names which confronts anyone running their eyes up and down a wine-shop shelf, we concentrated on grape varieties. Of the four elements which define a wine's flavour, these are the easiest to understand. We've now had a close look at sixteen of the most widely planted grape varieties, and a quick glimpse at 80 more. I hope you've plunged your corkscrew into a few bottles in the meantime, and begun the thoroughly satisfying process of putting flavours to names for yourself.

Now it's time to set off in a different direction. Grape varieties are, if you like, the genetic route to flavour; we're now going to take the geographical route to flavour. That, you'll recall from the beginning of the book, is wine's singular claim on our attention: it gives flavours to places on earth. We may not have the time or the money to be able to travel to see the graceful, sparse-limbed gum trees, bright nectar-sipping birds and operatic sunsets of the South Australian bush. For under £10, though, we can taste the ancient, burnt-red Australian earth and the dazzling fury of an Australian summer – in a glass of black McLaren Vale or Barossa Shiraz. Another £10 will bring you a ticket to the Rhine terraces on an autumn morning, with flavours as delicate and brilliant as dew-jewelled spider's webs.

Ten pounds more, and you can be in the south of France, where hills of white stone throw scent into the air through the fine-leaved medium of wiry thyme and woody rosemary.

You can, in other words, taste regions when you taste wines. Indeed, in all fairness, I should point out that wines usually taste more strongly of regions than they do of grape varieties. Let me return to a quotation I used in section 4, from the late Peter Sichel of Château Palmer. "A Cabernet Sauvignon from Bordeaux," he said, "bears more resemblance to a Merlot from Bordeaux than it does to a Cabernet Sauvignon from Australia or Chile; Meursault and Chablis are a better guide to the style of wine in the bottle than if both are labelled Chardonnay." Put another way, when you taste a memorable Barossa Shiraz you taste Barossa first and Shiraz second, and if you taste a fine bottle of Pomerol you taste Pomerol first and Merlot second. The ultimate truth of wine is geography.

That's why I'm now slipping a round-the-world ticket surreptitiously into your hand. The journey will be a bit longer and a bit more complicated than our initial stroll down the Avenue of Grape Varieties. But I hope you'll enjoy it. We'll start the tour in France, still the country which gives the world more interesting and complex wines than any other.

68 Bordeaux: sea songs

In wine-producing terms, Bordeaux is not so much a lake as an ocean. In a good year, it would produce about the same amount of wine as the whole of Australia, and rather more than the whole of Chile. Its wines are made from blends of at least five major grape varieties, with half-a-dozen more playing some sort of subsidiary role. Is it possible, then, to talk about 'the taste of Bordeaux'?

Not if you're a pedant, but pedants will already have discarded this book as inadequate. In all of the sections that follow, we're going to have to generalise very broadly about the sort of flavours that large tracts of land – sometimes even whole continents – provide. Yet there is a core of truth to these generalisations, as most drinkers will quickly realise after they've got themselves orientated. It's why you or I reach for one bottle on a shelf rather than another. So yes: Bordeaux does have its own taste.

If the entire spectrum of red wine occupied a target, I'd guess Bordeaux would be positioned somewhere near the middle, the bull's-eye. By this I don't mean that the Bordeaux style of red wine ought to be the model for which all red-wine makers the world over should aim; that would be a global catastrophe. I simply mean that its flavour is a sort of golden mean, a halfway house, for all the things red wine can possibly contain. Tannin, acid, fruit flavours, mineral or earthy flavours, overall weight: Bordeaux is just about in the middle, just about all the time. It's the ultimate mid-weight red. Hence, in the end, its popularity. It's like a political party which captures the centre ground so absolutely that it can't help getting elected.

Most Bordeaux reds are blends of Cabernet Sauvignon and Merlot, with lesser amounts of Cabernet Franc, Malbec and Petit Verdot. Its soils are often gravelly, with purer limestone and clays also playing a role; its climate is a warm maritime one, meaning that its summers are rarely burningly hot and its winters rarely chill enough to shatter statues, but that changeability is at all times a risk, a problem, a delight. Parts of Bordeaux, like the Médoc, are quite palpably places, gravelly places, where the sea meets the sky. Ships of land, if you like, edging nervously out into the Atlantic, bathed in soft, nacreous light. Vintages, therefore, make a big difference in Bordeaux, whereas (for example) in most parts of Chile they have little significance.

'Mid-weight', though, would hardly account for the passion which Bordeaux's red wines (known in Britain as clarets) inspire in its devotees. This is due to two factors: complexity and balance.

What's complexity? The sum total, to be mathematical about it, of an ample range of flavour notes to be found in a wine: there's rarely anything obvious or simple about the flavour of red Bordeaux, even a relatively cheap one. It's a wine with lots of different flavours meshed together, like the tiny dots of colour which go to make a pointillist painting. Those flavours can include currants, plums, raspberries, earth or stones, pencils, cedar and dark chocolate – as well as a couple of hundred more. I'll leave you the pleasure of discovering them all.

What's balance? This concerns the way all those flavours are attached to each other – the organisation of energy within a wine, if you like. There is something about Bordeaux's grapes in Bordeaux's ground beneath Bordeaux's sky which gives its wines intrinsic balance, and that balance is what helps a wine move through the mouth and satisfy the drinker after he or she has swallowed. It's also what helps a wine accompany food well, as Bordeaux's reds so memorably do.

Naturally there are sub-regional differences, too: wines from the Médoc tend to be brisk, pure and curranty; those from Pessac-Léognan and Graves softly earthy; those from St Emilion and Pomerol more creamy, plummy and meaty. In general, though, the bliss of red Bordeaux is its overall refinement, composition and even reticence of flavour, rather than the actual flavour triggers themselves. It is red wine of great subtlety. That

subtlety should be detectable even in the simplest of
its wines and everywhere evident in the greatest of
its wines.

Bad red Bordeaux, of which there is
unfortunately plenty, obviously fails to live up to any
of these lofty ambitions. Thinness and meanness of
flavour is its chief vice; hardness, grubbiness and
greenness are other failings. Sloppy winemaking and
over-high crop levels are the usual causes, but a cold
and rainy vintage may also be to blame.

The best of Bordeaux's dry whites are probably
France's most underrated fine wines: their creamy
oak richness is softly folded into gentle fruit and
vegetable flavours like whipped egg white into a
soufflé, giving soft, dappled whites of great grace.
Alas, they are uncommon: much dry white Bordeaux
is just thinnish, sharpish Sauvignon. Persevere,
though: the best do not always cost a great deal and,
even if the oak component is missing, good-quality
blends of dry Bordeaux Sauvignon and Sémillon can
create whites of exciting intrinsic complexity.

Much the same could be said of Bordeaux's
sweet whites. The best, few in number and high in
price, will astonish you with their succulence. I
couldn't believe how indecently rich and unctuous
the first great Sauternes I ever had the chance to
taste was (1976 Château de Malle, since you ask):
suddenly, I understood what that puzzling term
'lanolin' meant when attached to a wine description,
since this sweet wine seemed to ooze a rich yet clean
fattiness that one might well imagine being combed
out of wool freshly shaved from the back of a
bemused ewe. The intense sweetness of these wines
is balanced, though, by acidity and botrytis flavours,
and gently amplified by the lush vanillins of oak. By
definition, they are wines of low yields and high
sacrifice, which in turn means that any relatively
inexpensive sweet white wine from the Bordeaux

region is likely to be the result, more or less
unhappy, of a series of compromises. The best is well
worth the extra.

69
Burgundy: punting on a paradox

Unusually for France, the wines produced in
Burgundy are based on single grape varieties:
Chardonnay for white burgundy, and Pinot Noir for
red. Since we've already covered these grapes in
sections 51 and 59, won't that do, Miss?

This is the kind of suggestion that could get me
into a lot of trouble in cellars in Beaune or Nuits.
The idea that red burgundy might be a varietal Pinot
Noir, or white burgundy just another Chardonnay, is
heretical to a Burgundian. He or she would argue
that their wines taste as they do because of their
vineyard sites; the cultured labour invested in
growing the fruit; and the sun, clouds and rain to
which the fruit was exposed during a particular
vintage. Oh, and winemaking plays a part, too,
though it's not really as important as people think.
But grape variety? Never!

How, then, might the taste of white burgundy
differ from the taste of a Tom, Dick or Harry
Chardonnay plucked at random from a shelf of
yellow wines? Less fruit, for a start; and probably
less obvious oak. Fewer sweet edges; probably
higher acidity. Above all, there would be a sort of
sinewy quality to the wine, a chewiness, a vinosity,
which would give you the impression that it was well
structured.

If it was young, it might be a bit plain; you'd
poke around in it to find little details of aroma and
flavour, and maybe you wouldn't turn much up. A
quiet, blossom-like scent, perhaps; a whiff of pale

nuts; some delicate apple or grapefruit: little hints, just to tease. But its presence and weight in the mouth would somehow impress you nonetheless, and it would go reasonably well with food.

If it was older, it would probably give you a bit more. The volume button for those nuts would have been turned up, and there'd be a little of the butteriness which you're so familiar with in the rest of the world's oaked Chardonnays stealing in. A range of summer fruits – apricot, peach, nectarine – might be starting to show themselves, and there'd be a sense of incipient richness that reminds you of the thrill of getting up early on a summer's morning and seeing sunlight begin to cascade on to the chiselled facades of limestone buildings and across mown lawns. In the mouth, the wine would be chattier, too: retaining that sense of tautness and structure, yet filling in the gaps with deft dabs of softly buttered fruits.

That's the general idea, anyway, with lots of differences depending on sub-region (Chablis should be green and steely; Meursault relatively rich; Montagny chunky and straightforward; Mâcon-Villages soft and easy-going) and quality level (don't expect too much until you've paid around double what an ordinary Chilean Chardonnay would cost). Bad white burgundy is, above all, dull, mealy and inarticulate, though it may also be badly balanced (harsh and acidic) or grubby. In general, however, white burgundy is more consistent than red. If you love Chardonnay, then it's worth making an effort to explore white burgundy: you'll enjoy what it has to offer, and you won't get ripped off too often.

I wish I could say the same of red burgundy, which has for long been a wine of notorious and exasperating inconsistency. Rising winemaking standards, and a run of good vintages in the 1990s, have improved matters; the fact remains, though, that these are wines produced at the northern limits of red-wine production, and hence they are difficult and challenging. Every vintage is a tightrope act, and my own cellar (not, I'm sure, untypically) is littered with the bottled corpses of wines which got caught in the cross-winds, lost their balance, and crashed to the ground. From time to time I drink them, grumpily: another £30 down the drain. *Grand Cru*? Grand Con, more like.

Anyway, let's not get too lugubrious. In general, I think it's fair to say that most red burgundy is actually closer to varietal Pinot Noir than white burgundy is to international Chardonnay, though this may only be because there are fewer Pinot Noirs around to provide a comparison. Varietal Pinot Noir wines generally offer light, pure fruit, often suggesting cherries or currants or raspberries, and red burgundy starts from that point, too. In the case of cheap red burgundy, it stops there, and the fruit is generally rather chilly and sour. Pay a bit more, though, and ...

... and at best, you may stumble across something that amplifies those fruit notes to a remarkable degree, so that you begin to think that you've never really tasted cherries or currants or raspberries until this moment. The flavour echoes around you, like a trumpet voluntary played in a cathedral. Behind the fruit, there are other, more complex flavours – spices like cloves and liquorice; an earthiness; perhaps a roastiness or a smokiness; perhaps something more exotic, suggesting truffle or leather. Age will take these components and intermingle them, relaxing and unwinding them and bringing in new and sometimes more dangerous notes still – of undergrowth or decay. By the end of the process, the wine has become extraordinarily articulate and expressive, like a little mill of aromas and flavours to please and tantalise. There is, indeed, a sort of improbability about it altogether since, if you take the component parts (tannin, acidity, richness of flavour) of the wine to pieces in your mouth, it doesn't seem to add up to much, yet as a whole it is as powerful and stentorian as any wine you've ever come across. That's the paradox of red burgundy. Can't do it; won't do it; then does it anyway, dazzlingly. Once in a while.

Oh, and one last thing: Beaujolais. This is made from the Gamay grape variety (you might also come across something called Bourgogne-Passe-Tout-Grains, which is two-thirds Gamay, one-third Pinot Noir). Most Beaujolais has the colour and flavour notes of a red wine, but the texture and balance of a white: it's good chilled. The best Beaujolais should have a vivid and gulpable juiciness to it and, very occasionally (from cru appellations like Moulin-à-Vent or Morgon), it can have some meaty substance, too. The one thing Beaujolais should never be is *serious*.

Champagne: the silvery edge

Ah, the problems of success! Champagne has been so successful in promoting itself and its image that no one treats it as a wine anymore. It's a social marker, a symbolic lubricant: the sort of thing you drink at all those moments when the last thing you're thinking about is what you're drinking. But what does it actually taste like?

Vomit. That, anyway, was my first tasting note for it, jointly identified with my brother Michael when we were in our early teens and were given a taste every time the moon turned blue. Real Champagne tastes of vomit. Despite that, we quite liked it. Indeed we like it to this day.

Champagne is very acidic, of course, and this was what Mick and I had correctly identified; that acidity reminded us of the taste of gastric reflux. You could very well call this the taste of its region. Champagne is the most northerly of all France's vineyard areas, which means that it's very cool. Most of it is a blend of three grape varieties: Chardonnay, plus the red Pinot Noir and Pinot Meunier grapes made as white wines (without skins). If you were to taste any of these as still white wines, before they've been blended and sparkled, your mouth would pucker with horror: they're sour, sour, sour. That anything even semi-palatable can be made out of them at all seems a surprise, let alone a wine as memorable and delicious as Champagne can be.

Once it's been through the alchemical process of blending and secondary fermentation, that sourness has become a deliciously crisp and sabre-like edge. The texture of the bubbles, plus the flavours of secondary fermentation itself, of yeast lees and of the little tinkle of sweetness which goes in at the very end of the process, all provide the softly biscuity counterbalance to that crispness. Age, meanwhile, has liberated all sorts of other surprising aromas and smells in the wine which were hidden away under the snowdrift of acidity at an earlier stage: flowers, fruits, leaves. The wine swarms through the mouth, all vivacity and intensity, leaving it feeling fresh and invigorated – and ready for more.

That silvery edge of acidic incision is what distinguishes Champagne from all other sparkling wines, and the key to it, once again, is Champagne's place on earth and its chalky soils (pure forms of limestone always seem to help produce wines with some sort of blade about their person). Other regions can only mimic Champagne's acidity by picking their grapes early, thus slightly underripe – and underripe grapes never acquire a full spectrum of flavours.

Champagne's are both fully ripe and yet highly acidic. The most serious challengers to its hegemony, therefore, come from those areas that can duplicate such conditions, like southern England, New Zealand's South Island, or Tasmania.

How about different styles and qualities of Champagne? Cheap Champagne is often coarse, green and raw; bargains, alas, are few. The vast majority of Champagnes are non-vintage, which means, in effect, a blend of different vintages, and here standards vary greatly: the famous names – Moët et Chandon, Lanson, Veuve Clicquot and so on – generally offer consistency, albeit at a premium (due to the fact that we have to pay for their ludicrous advertising campaigns), well chosen own-label non-vintage Champagne from supermarkets and chain stores can offer better value, though the bottle doesn't quite carry the same social cachet. Among the famous names, house styles provide slight variations (Veuve Clicquot and Roederer are relatively richly flavoured, for example; Lanson is very crisp; Pommery delicate).

If you greatly enjoy Champagne and want to discover how complex it can be, experiment with vintage Champagnes. These are a selection of the top wines of one year only, and usually offer the best quality/price ratio of any Champagne product. They also age well, too: aged Champagne loses some of its crispness and edge, and its sparkle softens, but in return you get rich aromas and flavours of autumn dessert apples and walnut butter. If you have ideal storage conditions, Champagne can be aged for ten or fifteen years.

The very top Champagnes are called *cuvées de prestige* (prestige blends); they're usually more intense than everything else, but not by much, and certainly not by as much as the price jump above ordinary vintage Champagne. Glam status symbols, though, if you're into that kind of thing.

Blanc de Blancs Champagne is made from Chardonnay grapes alone; it can and should be exceptionally fine-grained and delicate. Blanc de Noirs is made from black grapes: not heavier but more richly fruited, sometimes with a distinctive rooty aroma. Most rosé Champagne is made by blending a little still red into lots of white, so it tastes less different from ordinary Champagne than you'd expect. It's still worth hunting around for discreet little whiffs of strawberry, though the real pleasure of it is in the colour itself.

Brut Champagne is dryish, though not as dry as Extra Brut or Brut Nature. Extra Dry, Sec, Demi-Sec and Rich or Doux are progressively sweeter.

71
Alsace: blossom on the wind

Alsace is easy. In one sense, anyway: it's the only part of France that not only makes almost all its wines from single grape varieties but labels them in that way, too. It has a palpable regional style and many of its best vineyard sites are flagged by the words 'Grand Cru' on the label. Alsace wines aren't always faultless, of course, but, in general, winemaking standards are relatively high and the region is home to some of France's few truly excellent cooperative wineries. Any problems at all, then?

Just one. It's hard to know how sweet the wine you've just bought is going to be.

Most Alsace wines are dry, but the regional style is very much for the well rounded white. Such wines seem consonant with the place: almost fictitiously pretty medieval villages nestling beneath wooded slopes on the sunny, lee side of the Vosges mountains; fountains babbling among geraniums in

the village square; a confetti of fruit blossom
tumbling past your hotel window when the wind gets
up in April. The vines up on the kaleidoscopic soils
of the hillside have the fullness of buns, of pears, of
sacks of grain. Softly spicy fruit packs them. Packs
them so full, indeed, that they can drift away from
dryness towards sweetness, seemingly without the
producer realising it. Sometimes the drinker is
alerted by the phrases *vendange tardive* (late harvest)
or *séléction des grains nobles* (selection of botrytis-
affected berries) on the label, but just as often there
is nothing to hint at the fact that your bottle of Pinot
Gris may actually be too sweet to accompany the
fillet of sea bass you've just ordered, or the oysters
which your husband is attempting so dangerously to
open at the moment. My own strategy is to save
Alsace wines for white meats, which they partner
well, even if the wine proves slightly sweet.

Of the different varieties, Riesling and Muscat
(strangely enough) are the two driest. Riesling,
indeed, can almost approach austerity: its capacity
for absorbing and concentrating (or mimicking)
mineral flavours can give it the incipient hardness of
purified ore in Alsace. Its fruit qualities, too, scour
the mouth, especially when young; don't be put off,
though, for these can be fine, deep-driving, oak-free
whites of genuine profundity. Muscat d'Alsace smells
very sweet, but tastes much dryer than its scent
would suggest.

This pair contrasts with (in increasingly buxom
order) Pinot Blanc, Pinot Gris and Gewürztraminer,
which vary from plump to positively matronly, with
various levels of smokiness and spiciness bringing
complexity within their generally low-acid frame.
Sylvaner, should you see it, is plainer but often a
good food choice, since it tends to have slightly
higher acidity; Auxerrois is a grape variety commonly
blended with, and sold under the name of, Pinot

Blanc. The only example I've ever tried reminded me (though it was a decade old at the time) of white chocolate and strawberries. Edelzwicker is the local name for a blend of varieties; since in Alsace the blend is considered inferior to the varietal, the fruit used is generally unexciting in quality. Pinot Noir is Alsace's pale, wan red, and Crémant d'Alsace its sometimes impressive sparkling wine.

72 The Loire: watermoods

Was ever the name of a river more riverine than the Loire? That long, slow, single syllable seems to unwind in such a liquid and leisurely manner that it's hard to be put in mind of anything other than a wide stretch of water curling though pastureland and parks, eddying beneath the sculpted arches of châteaux, or drifting amiably past the spore-filled caves of mushroom growers.

The wines of the Loire, too, seem to reflect the moods and caprices of France's longest river, to such an extent that you wonder if it can be purely accidental or if, by contrast, the river itself in some mysterious way has penetrated the local spirit of agricultural endeavour. The two extremes provide flavours of sometimes austere dryness and freshness. Sancerre and Pouilly-Fumé, sited about halfway down the river's trajectory, are the places on earth where the Sauvignon Blanc grape reaches its most stonily pungent form, echoed in nearby appellations like Menetou-Salon and Sauvignon de Touraine: dream whites for a trout or a pike. By contrast, Muscadet and Gros Plant, the Loire's last wines as it begins to grow estuarine and salty, seem to be the companions oysters and shellfish long for as they head for masticatory oblivion. The white-almond aromas and steel-edged, lemony neutrality of these wines, sometimes gently textured and breaded with a little yeast, serves exactly the same function as the chunk of lemon the waiter nestles in the centre of your *plateau des fruits de mer*.

Between tumbling down out of the Massif Central and dissolving in the Atlantic brine, the Loire makes a very lazy, slow-moving journey through 'the garden of France' (*le jardin de la France*). The wines produced along this stretch are utterly different in character from the fish-eagle whites of Sancerre and the oyster-catchers of Muscadet. The white wines of Vouvray, Anjou and other local appellations, most of them from the Chenin Blanc rather than the Sauvignon Blanc variety, are, in general, much fuller and more statuesque. They can be very dry, too, but many of them are medium dry or sweet, brimming with honey, wax, peach, quince and dessert apple aromas and flavours. What they nearly always have is relatively high acidity to balance out, redeem and freshen their sweetness. The best age superbly, both dry and sweet. Cheap, poor-quality examples, though, tend to stink of sulphur and taste of raw apple cores.

It's warm and mellow enough in Saumur and Anjou for red wines, too, produced from the Cabernet Franc grape variety; the two best-known appellations are Chinon and Bourgeuil. There's an inky, pungent freshness and briskness to these wines, with lively acidity and an iron-like streak behind their juicy, raspberry fruits. They lunge out of the glass, and have a short way with tender lamb. When unsuccessful, though, they're green, grassy and sharp.

73

The Rhône: a river of two halves

'Comforting', perhaps that's the word. 'Warm' would be another; 'savoury' a third. The wines of the Rhône have usually been thought country cousins to those of Bordeaux and Burgundy: reds to relax and have fun with when you're tired of the over-polished restraint of claret and the exasperating parsimoniousness of burgundy. In fact, as the last two decades have shown, the Rhône's finest wines can be as mouth-dazzlingly good as anything else produced in France – as well as, of course, depressing as deeply as the worst wines of those other regions, when the vintage was cool and wet or the winemaking incompetent.

The Rhône divides neatly into two halves. The northern Rhône (which includes wines like Hermitage, Côte-Rôtie, Cornas, St Joseph and Crozes-Hermitage) is where the Syrah grape variety feels most at home, reaching levels of intensity and expressivity achieved nowhere else on earth. At best, these are red wines of great aromatic power. Their Syrah scent washes over you like a wave: sheer, drenching, exuberant. It might remind you of fruits like blackcurrant, blackberry or mulberry; there will probably be sense of creamy, sheeny, wash-day freshness to it; you might catch a hint of violets or other flowers in it, and maybe a whiff of hot rubber, too. With age, the wines become more savoury, more animal: the sort of scents you might catch in proximity to horses or cows or by handling riding tackle, yet that creaminess, excitingly, remains. The flavours of young northern Rhône reds can be very bright, fresh and juicy, with more blackcurrant and blackberry, backed up with liquorice and chocolate; again, with age there is a process of melting down into something softer, suppler and richer, suggesting leather or truffle yet retaining its fruit definition nonetheless. Bad northern Rhône reds are sharp and acid – and even in good ones, you should expect a bolt of acidity running through them like a spinal cord.

The reds of the southern Rhône, by contrast, tend to be based on other grape varieties, most notably Grenache but also Cinsault and Mourvèdre as well as Syrah. A warmer climate and different range of soil types (Rhône valley soils, in general, are highly diverse) provides fatter, richer, softer and sweeter wines than in the northern Rhône, smelling of raisins and toffee and tasting chewy, luscious, even soupy and sometimes 'hot' with high alcohol levels. Châteauneuf-du-Pape is the classic, but Lirac, Gigondas and Costières de Nîmes, as well as the best of the ordinary Côtes du Rhône and its 'Villages', can provide these sensations. Higher proportions of Syrah in a blend will freshen the wine up and lend it edge and definition. Bad southern Rhône reds are big, brainless and boring.

What about whites? Again, the Rhône divides into two – but not so much geographically, this time, as by variety. Viognier, that rising star among white grapes, has its home in the Condrieu appellation in the northern Rhône. Condrieu is always expensive, alas, but it remains one of the most extraordinary white wines on earth, both smelling and tasting of a sort of exotic compost of flowers, with glycerous, thick-textured peachy fruit. Despite its high price and prestige, it's best drunk young.

The rest of the Rhône valley's white wines are generally based on blends of Marsanne and Roussanne; in the south, other varieties, like Grenache Blanc, Bourboulenc, Clairette and Picpoul, come into the picture. I wouldn't worry about these names, though, since the basic style is similar: fat, full, chunky though rather inarticulate wines, with gentle pear or apricot fruit, generally going well with food but not leaving you with any sense of clear personality afterwards. They're a good choice if you're fed up with the shrill, high-acid screech of Sauvignon Blanc or Muscadet, or if you find Australian, Chilean or Californian Chardonnay undrinkably bright, noisy and over-oaked.

The Rhône's very best whites, though, from the Hermitage or Châteauneuf-du-Pape appellations, can rival great white burgundy with their dry, viscous richness and haunting presence. They smell intoxicatingly of white blossom and spring hedgerows (hawthorn and Queen Anne's lace, for those who have walked England's country lanes in May), and taste powerful yet subtle, too, of summer fruits, nuts and (once again) tiny white flowers. Unlike Viognier-based whites, too, they age superbly.

74 The Rest of France: curiouser and curiouser

In many ways, southern France is the most exciting wine-producing area in the world at present. Why? Because of endeavour. It's a little lesson, if you like, in the importance of not giving up.

Thirty years ago, southern France was a wine-producing disaster area. Huge swathes of vines sprawled across the coastal plains like green lava. These unloved plants produced cheap, harsh wine sold in plastic-capped refillable litre bottles that no one wanted any longer. The days when French workers looked like Jean Gabin, smoked untipped Gauloises, passed doomed days in grimy railway yards and drank half-a-litre of rough red with every meal including breakfast were over.

There were two ways forward. Both have been

tried; both work. And, to get back to our point, both provide a different range of flavours.

The first is easy enough to discover: *vins de pays*. This little phrase means 'country wines'. Initially, they were meant to be the first rung up the ladder leading to appellation contrôlée status – to their becoming grown-up wines, as it were. Since their geographical names were in the main unrecognizable, they were allowed to put, as a special treat, the grape variety names on their labels. And guess what?

You got it: they've been a steaming international success. Precisely because they had grape-variety names on their labels – names, in other words, which consumers could relate to and felt comfortable with. The actual Vins de Pays name has become less and less important as time has gone by – most producers now simply use the basic overall name covering most of the region, which is Vins de Pays d'Oc, even though there are dozens of more specific, local names to choose from.

It's affected the taste of the wines, too. Most Vins de Pays no longer taste like apprentice AOC wines; they taste like New World wines made in France. Indeed, they're often made by Australians, New Zealanders or Californians, or by French winemakers who have trained in those regions. They're sound, fruity, safe and reliable. In general, the style is faithful to its grape variety, often with greater freshness and liveliness than the sometimes heavy, overdrawn varietals of the New World. They tend, too, to have a typically French, easy-drinking balance to them and, when they're oaked, this is done with restraint. The best have vivid depth of fruit; the worst (and there are plenty of these) are yawnfully dull.

That was one way forward, and very profitable it's proved, too. More difficult to understand but, in the end, far more interesting to drink are those wines which have appellation contrôlée status, wine sold under names like Corbières, Minervois, Coteaux du Languedoc, Coteaux d'Aix-en-Provence, Côtes du Roussillon and, north-west towards the Pyrenees, Madiran, Cahors, Côtes du Saint-Mont, Jurançon and Pacherenc du Vic Bilh. They're more difficult not only because of the unfamiliarity of their names but also because they're often made using blends of regional, not international, grape varieties. Yet they often connect back with deep-rooted traditions in their areas. These, in other words, were the wines developed over hundreds of years of slow viticultural evolution, the wines which best let the soils and the hillsides of these forgotten corners of France speak. When made with modern levels of viticultural care and winemaking know-how, they can be extremely impressive: dark reds with floral, earthy or herby scents and thick-textured flavours which might remind you of stones, fire and minerals. (Less successful wines can be spiky and hard.) The whites are less memorable: most are well balanced and food-friendly but only mildly characterful. Wines made from the Petit Manseng grape variety (like Jurançon and Pacherenc) are an exception to this rule: they are slender but intense and perfumed when dry, and vividly honeysuckle-like when sweet. There are, too, some strong and heady rosés, particularly from Languedoc and Provence.

Little, yet, from this region is very expensive; much is rewarding and satisfying. Even if you don't recognise the name, try the wine; you might be pleasantly surprised.

Finally, a couple of French footnotes, probably more familiar to walkers or skiers than drinkers: the Jura and Savoie. Both of these regions have long winegrowing traditions, which means a legacy of complicated names and unusual specialities (like the Jura's bizarre and expensive *vin jaune*). The key feature of many of the Jura's whites is deliberate partial oxidation; it gives them what seems at first to be rather a tired style, which later may strike you as a complex and engaging nutty note; the Jura's reds are generally very pale, but can be smooth and haunting.

Savoies's whites are, as you'd expect, mountain-fresh, full of aerial grace – but on occasion surprisingly richly flavoured. The reds are dark, lively and fresh, sometimes with mineral overtones.

75

Spain: an end to drowsiness

A guitar chord; a donkey standing motionless in the furnace of midday; a stadium where you can choose to sit in sun or shade to watch death enacted before you, at five in the afternoon. The list could go on: dancers able to convey a history of sorrow with a click of their heels; storks nesting, to extravagantly public effect, at the top of church towers; the little pieces of paper on which tapas are served blowing down gloomy alleyways early on a Sunday morning, as the last reveller goes home to bed and the first widow steps out to mass. And wine, of course ... soft, pale red wine, wine that has slumbered for years in old oak casks, tottering gently out of your glass and down your throat amid wafts of vanilla.

Spain, I've always thought, is more uncomplicatedly itself than any other European country, its national identity as much a settled part of the landscape as any mountain or lake. For decades, Spanish wine changed little: dull white, muscular rosé, and drowsy, throat-soothing reds which all seemed to want to be venerable Rioja if they could. There was an international affection for Spanish wine, but it was based more strongly on holiday memories and modest prices than on ingrained excellence.

Not any more. Spanish wine is now excitingly diverse. What are some of its key flavours?

Rioja remains Spain's classic: soft-textured, well rounded, Tempranillo-based red wine, with medium depth of colour and scents and flavours of vanilla and strawberry, tobacco and plum. It's cleaner and fresher than it used to be; deeper, too; and often with more innate complexity (due to better winemaking and increased use of French as well as American oak casks). In neighbouring Navarra, the style is generally similar, but greater use of grape varieties like Cabernet Sauvignon gives the fruit a slightly brisker, more curranty style. Valdepeñas, although geographically removed from Rioja, continues to offer the pale, trembly reds of distant tradition. White Rioja trails red for interest, but the cleaner, fresher, modern approach has made it more drinkable than the tired, oxidised standard of the past. Barrel-fermentation techniques, too, are beginning to create some excitingly creamy, supple white Riojas.

Softness is still the hallmark of other Spanish reds, but increased use of international grape varieties and more ambitious winemaking has broadened the picture considerably. Spain, whose climate in general is both warmer and more reliable than that of either France or Italy, is the European country with more potential to meet competition from Australia and Chile than any other. Indeed, when I was last in Australia, the rumour was that growers throughout the whole of La Mancha, the largest tract of vineyard in the world, were to be allowed to graft their indifferent Airén vines over to any other variety they wished. If true, this would provide the largest new plantings of international varieties Europe has ever seen. The Australians were worried.

As it is, winemaking advances are bringing excitingly dark reds to Calatayud and Cariñena, Murcia and Jumilla, Toro and, especially, Ribera del Duero: you might catch scents and flavours of blackberry and plum in these wines, with other notes of oak and tar and, often, the effortlessly high alcohol levels which come, here, with full grape ripeness (as in much of Australia). Penedés, Conca de Barberá and Somontano are all, at least in part, higher-sited vineyard areas bringing more edge and definition to fruit flavours, with widespread use of international varieties like Cabernet Sauvignon, Merlot and Pinot Noir. Priorato is an extraordinary area whose generally high-priced wines are always strong and intense, their flavours varying from coffee, tobacco and herbs to something downright medicinal.

Among whites, styles vary from taut and crisp (Rueda) to thoroughly international in style, like the softly lemony, oaked Chardonnay produced in Somontano, Penedés and Costers del Segre. Perhaps Spain's most distinctive white-wine style comes from Galicia, that damp, green land which lies above northern Portugal on Iberia's western edge. Whites here, most notably from the Albariño grape variety, have a fresh delicacy which seems altogether un-Spanish. Their scents and flavours of honeysuckle, peach and apricot have proved so popular that prices for these wines are high.

Cava, finally: the world's biggest selling sparkling wine. Most Cava is well made, consistent but fundamentally unambitious. At best, it has a gentle, soft and flowery character; its fruit notes recall apple and lemon. At worst, it has a coarse rawness.

76
Jerez and Sherry: the peacock's tail

Sherry deserves a section to itself. There's nothing else like it; and it's fine. Indeed of all the world's great wines, it is the most neglected and overlooked – and the least expensive. There are, in other words, lots of reasons to take sherry seriously.

In addition to that, it's what one might call an alchemical wine: it transmutes base matter into gold.

The grape variety used to make sherry is called Palomino. Ordinary white wine made from Palomino is ... well, ordinary. Bland, mild, unexceptional, it's a Mr Average grape variety. Give it the sherry treatment, and it pulls on a suit of lights, acquiring a range of unique, intense and glittering flavours. How?

By two strategies for ageing the wines: biological and chemical. The biological means is the most mysterious. Dry Palomino wine is lightly fortified and then set to age in part-empty barrels. The 'sherry triangle' (the towns of Jerez de la Frontera, Sanlúcar de Barrameda and Puerto de Santa María) faces the Gulf of Cádiz, and the moist air inhaled off the sea by the hot, high, mountainous heart of Spain draws with it spores of yeast moulds, which colonise the wine, forming a whitish carpet over its surface. This blanket of mould is called *flor* or 'flower'. It's most active in spring and autumn and dies away in summer and winter.

It is *flor*, rather than Palomino wine, that provides the chief flavour notes in fino sherry: that pungent, bread-like freshness, that mouthwatering, faintly bitter keenness, that sense of a slicing edge to the wine, yet one achieved with low levels of acidity. 'Manzanilla' is a fino which comes from Sanlúcar de Barrameda alone: it has a particularly soft and supple character, like the very freshest of breads.

We'll be looking at food and wine matching

more closely later, in Part Six, but it's worth noting here that few wines have been more underrated by the British, gastronomically speaking, than fino sherry. It's usually served in tiny glasses, at room temperature, from a bottle that's been open a month or two. It should be served in large glasses, with a meal, straight out of the fridge, from a bottle that's been open no more than a day or two. Repeated experiment has satisfied me that no wine on earth makes a better all-purpose food match than chilled fino sherry. When I quit wine-writing and can go back to drinking what I want, fino sherry will be the white wine I drink more than any other.

So much for private passions. What about the other way of turning boring Palomino into exciting sherry? The chemical way?

'Chemical' sounds sinister. In fact, though, it simply means using oxidation (described in section 29) to age fortified Palomino wine. Oxidation is a chemical rather than a biological process – hence the name. The effects of air on these dull wines, especially when combined with the commingling of older and younger components that the solera system (see page 213) provides, is to give them dark colours and powerful, reeky aromas and flavours, often described as 'nutty' (think of walnuts). They also remind the drinker of dried apricots and, more metaphorically, varnishes and polishes, evoking (maybe happily, maybe not) the smell of long-forgotten schoolrooms. The name for such a sherry would be 'dry oloroso'.

Of course, that's far from the end of the story. There's another sherry style called 'amontillado', which, technically, is meant to be an old fino that's finished its life under flor and has begun ageing oxidatively, giving the drinker a lighter, more fine-grained alternative to oloroso. (From Sanlúcar comes 'manzanilla pasada' – an old manzanilla, just before it begins to become an amontillado.) 'Palo cortado' is another median style: lighter, more fragrant and more gently articulated than oloroso.

Everything I've described so far is dry, and sometimes tongue-drivingly so, but dry sherries are often mixed with sweetening wines (traditionally made from the Pedro Ximénez grape variety) to give medium-dry or sweet styles; the latter are termed 'creams'. The quality of cheap cream sherries, including big brands and the so-called 'pale creams' (a bastard mixture of fino or very light amontillado with concentrated must), is so mediocre that it might seem tempting to dismiss all sweet sherry. Taste, though, some of the ancient dessert sherries of traditional houses like González Byass or Valdespino and you'll find enough wealth and spendour of flavour in them to silence criticism. These are peacocks of the wine world: their flavours unfold and fan out in the mouth, with quivering splendour, for minutes.

Montilla-Moriles is a separate district of Spain, lying further inland near Córdoba, but producing a similar range of sherry-like wines, both *flor*-aged and oxidatively aged. The main differences are that Pedro Ximénez is more widely used in Montilla than Palomino (indeed much of Jerez's sweetening wine comes from Montilla), and that Montilla wine is naturally so high in alcohol that it doesn't require fortification. In flavour terms, dry Montilla tends to be lighter and more delicate than sherry, and often offers extraordinarily good value for money.

77
Portugal: explorer's wines

Historically, the words 'Portugal' and 'exploration' have gone hand-in-hand. Before our world was charted, sea-dreaming Portuguese drew off from their home ports with perplexing readiness, risking all in voyages over the edge of the horizon.

In wine terms, too, the words go together. Portugal isn't easy: its grape varieties are unfamiliar, and their flavours unusual. If you're a wine explorer, though, you'll enjoy this shy, unassuming, culturally rich country.

Whites first. You probably already know Vinho Verde: 'green wine' grown in the damp and steamy Minho (the nearest Europe ever gets to rainforest) in the north of the country. Vines are everywhere here, but vineyards less common: most of the grapes are garden-grown, their vines providing trellised shade for peas and beans, potatoes and goose-necked cabbages, plus the occasional meditative and recalcitrant goat. Most Vinho Verde is low in alcohol, lively and refreshing – decidedly green and appley in flavour, but often slightly sweetened (and gas-prickled) for export purposes. The best is less green, riper and more flowery, made from the Alvarinho grape variety (which we met in Spain as Albariño).

In Portugal itself, however, most 'green wine' is red. Red Vinho Verde is the strangest wine I've ever drunk: dark yet slender and sharp, like acidic ink. It is the ultimate sardine wine, should you ever find yourself in front of the ultimate sardine (a fat fellow, swimming happily two hours earlier, now grilled over wooden twigs on a beach).

Portugal's other whites can be divided into those produced from international varieties like Chardonnay, and those produced from key Portuguese varieties. The international set are relatively subtle and nuanced in style, and usually worth a try – though I would always prefer something genuinely Portuguese.

The main problem facing Portugal's native whites is that they are all produced in areas where

the red wines attract more attention – like Douro,
Bairrada and Dão. The Bical grape variety in
Bairrada and the Encruzado in Dão can both
produce gently lemony whites that take well to oak,
while the Arinto grape variety tends to produce
wines that taste of green apples in the north and sour
butter in the south (especially Bucelas). The best
Portuguese white grape variety is probably Fernão
Pires (also called Maria Gomes) which, when well
made, has an interestingly musky fragrance and soft,
subtly aromatic flavour, like a distant Portuguese
echo of the better Rhône valley whites.

I suppose we ought to mention rosé in passing
since, in financial terms, it has certainly been
Portugal's greatest hit over the last 50 years. Mateus
Rosé and Lancers have provided an easy and
enjoyable route into wine for millions of drinkers,
and so much the better. These easy-going, sweetish
wines are, though, thoroughly international in style,
and their success has had more to do with historical
factors and marketing strategies than anything
specifically Portuguese.

If you want the real Portugal, you need to get
stuck into a few reds. This was sometimes hard work
in the past, since the Portuguese taste was for boot-
tough wines that would carry on ageing through
pestilence and nuclear attack to judgement day.
Bairrada and Dão were the worst offenders, and
there is sometimes still a tannic, acidic rigidity about
the reds from these two regions. Others, though,
combine an appealing grip with plenty of brisk, spicy
fruit, sometimes with overtones of tobacco, dust or
incense. They take well to new oak. Above all, they
are complex and well balanced and, with age, can
sometimes startlingly come to resemble wines from
that other part of Europe's Atlantic coastline,
Bordeaux.

The Douro, too, is a superb red-wine

producing region – or rather it would be if all the best fruit didn't get turned into port (see next section). Fine native varieties like Touriga Nacional produce Douro reds which combine a dense yet soft-textured earthiness with classically sweet, curranty fruit. Spain's Tempranillo, up in the Douro, is called Tinta Roriz, and the hot climate produces full-bodied, sweet-fruited, beefy reds redeemed by a vivid streak. How seriously will table-wine production be taken in the future in the Douro? World-class reds could reward those prepared to pursue them uncompromisingly and, for consumers, a trial purchase is usually worthwhile – though some reds from this region can still be tough, stalky, sour and uninspiring.

Southern Portugal, too, has much to offer, though in general the style of the reds there is much softer, rounder and sometimes more juicily fruity than further north. The problem here is the wine grower's poverty trap: low consumer expectations mean low prices; low prices put high quality out of reach. Yet the best red wines of regions like the Alentejo can be impressively soft and supple yet complex and rewarding, with lots of warm-fleshed, damsony fruit and effortless drinking balance.

Inter-regional blends are as much a Portuguese tradition as they are an Australian tradition, and Portuguese branded reds can be excellent, with the depth and complexity typical of the country at its best. If you're a fan of older wines, look out for the word *garrafeira*, which signifies extra bottle ageing before sale. Portugal also offers a superb, well aged, fortified sweet white Moscatel de Setúbal, which not only looks orange in colour but smells and tastes of oranges and tangerines, too.

78 The Douro and Port: beyond the mountains

Let's start with an aside. If you're interested in wine tourism, there are three areas of the viticultural world which strike me as being exceptionally beautiful, and which you should visit if you can. The Douro Valley, in northern Portugal, is the first of these; we'll come to the other two a little later.

The best way to get there is to take the orange diesel train which leaves Oporto for Pinhao. You'll cross the Douro river, just before it slides over its sandbar into the Atlantic, then chug entertainingly through the green, back-garden intimacies of the Minho. After that – and this is where our aside becomes more relevant – you tunnel your way through the Sierra de Marão, the mountain range which divides the Minho from the Douro.

Suddenly you're in a different landscape altogether: one fashioned by dry continental heat, rather than maritime moisture. All the clouds which come sliding off the Atlantic unburden themselves over Oporto, the Minho or, finally, on the slopes of the Marão. That, in brief, is why Vinho Verde is a slender green wine, while vintage port, just an hour away, is the world's darkest, most ferociously energetic wine: a black thunderclap of flavour.

The train journey gets more exciting, too. The valley drops away beneath you (I've opened the door and sat on the steps in the past), while the river stretches away, brim-full: it is, now, a series of dams. As you pull further into wine country, the hillsides begin to organise themselves into terraces, and the landscape takes on an exotic look, like an Iberian dream of Indian tea-gardens. The hillsides grow higher; the river narrows; you may see a kingfisher diving for cover as the train hoots mournfully to clear its rails of home-bound walkers with their shopping or their washing on their heads. Eventually, a dazed hour or so later, you pull into Pinhão, whose plentiful dogs scatter at the train's approach. The railway station greets you with blue tiled pictures of wine-harvest scenes to which, of course, the other passengers pay no attention whatsoever. Port's greatest farms (or *quintas*) stretch up in the blue haze about you, rising hundreds of feet in the air. It's a long way from home.

Port, as we discovered in section 27, is made by fortifying wine halfway through its fermentation. Most port is red, but you can make it with white grapes, too: white port is usually off-dry to sweet, and tastes mild, slippery, heady, faintly nutty. There is no more treacherous apéritif in the world, especially when served with superb Douro almonds and home-cured raw ham: it slides down so easily that you forget, until you fumble embarrassingly yet hilariously over your fork, how strong it is.

There are two port families: the ruby family and the tawny family. The ruby family goes through most of its ageing process in neutral containers or glass bottles: it's black to red in colour, often grippy in texture, sometimes smells of dry tea leaves and is plummy and peppery in flavour. The tawny family is aged in casks, where it oxidises very gently: it's pale red to amber or even walnut in colour, and tastes smooth and tangy, of dried fruits like apricot and fig with honey and caramel.

Each family has different quality (and price) levels: basic tawny, which is usually just a mixture of red and white port, is followed by ports in different age categories (10 years old, 20 years old and so on); vintage-dated tawny is called 'colheita' port. Basic ruby is followed by vintage character, late-bottled vintage and finally (best of all) vintage port. Vintage ports can either be sold under the name of the producing house (such as Dow or Taylor) or under the name of a single farm (Quinta do Bomfim, for example, or Quinta de Vargellas). The former are usually better than the latter, within the parameters of any given house style.

In my opinion, inexpensive ports offer good value for money, while expensive ports are less reliably exciting. The best of these, though, are uniquely magnificent, without parallel in the wine world: complex, resonant and allusive, with the ability to suggest the thunderous yet hidden vegetal power of nature in their youth, while becoming much calmer and more well ordered yet still engorged with sweet grandeur after a spell in the cellar.

Don't worry too much about all the ageing and decanting mystique. In principle, only vintage port is likely to improve with further storing once sold by the shipper, and this is almost the only port which has to be decanted (bottles of 'traditional' late-bottled vintage will also need decanting). Decanting itself just means pouring the wine from the bottle into another container (a jug, if you like), slowly and carefully, stopping as soon as you see any sign of the sediment flowing out of the bottle; it helps to stand the bottle up for a few days first. How old you drink your vintage port is up to you; I like them between 10 and 20 years old, with a little of the fire and passion of youth still clinging to them. Others consider that too young.

79
Madeira: rock of ages

Madeira is one of geography's great improbables: a fertile mountain top adrift in an ocean.

Its wine, too, pushes at the boundaries of probability. It came into being as an extension of the ship's chandlery which, willy-nilly, such pimples on the face of the sea must provide: wine for thirsty sailors deprived of recreation amid immensities of blue. In the end, paradoxically, it was the long equatorial journeys that its wines were forced to undergo which gave them their character. Madeira wine, in other words, is abused and maltreated – and much the better for it.

Abused and maltreated? The wines stowed away in those ships bound for the East Indies would have been exposed to heat, air and constant movement. Most wines would have been annihilated by this treatment; Madeira's wines, strangely enough, emerged from it as butterflies emerge from pupae.

Modern Madeira is both heated and oxidised before it becomes itself. This combination, indeed, is known as 'maderisation' – after Madeira. Only the shaking and rolling of a wallowing ship is no longer duplicated in Madeira production.

Ordinary, basic, commodity Madeira is cooked in giant, heated vats called *estufas*, before being aged in old wooden casks and vats. Top-quality Madeira, by contrast, is simply placed in old oak casks that are then stored in hot attics: the warm torpor of repeated Madeiran summers 'cooks' them slowly, gently and craftily. Time is, quite literally, Madeira's essence: vintage Madeira can't even be sold before it's twenty years old, and it then lasts almost as long as anybody wants to keep it. Having weathered this extraordinary process of attrition, little further can harm it.

Vintage Madeira is, in tasting terms, the most extraordinary wine I know. It has hugely powerful aromas, capable of suggesting anything from eggs and cheese through antique furniture to intense scents of dried fruit and nuts. Sipped, it is an essence: little drops flower on the tongue, then seem almost to take root there, twisting and turning and expanding until your whole mouth fills with flavour. Exactly what these flavours remind you of depends on the grape variety – and grape variety dictates sweetness. Sercial is dryest, sometimes austerely and raspingly so; Verdelho is medium dry, suggesting apples, grapes and walnuts. Bual is sweet and Malmsey very sweet – yet Madeira's uniformly high acidity levels and cask 'bite' means that these are never cloying wines. Instead, their apricot, raisin and fig sweetness is relieved and lifted by apple, grape and lemon – and essence of old stave. Thimblefuls of vintage Madeira provide a satisfactorily dazzling portion and, once opened, the bottle will keep for months. This is by way of saying that its apparent expense is, to some extent, chimerical.

Most Madeira is, sadly, not of vintage quality, but sold by age categories, the better of which are '5 years old', '10 years old' and '15 years old'. Madeira without any age statement is liable to be young, freshly cooked, simple and primitive in flavour, while no grape variety description means that the wine will be made from Tinta Negra Mole grapes – Madeira's own all-purpose, chameleon variety. This is not, in itself, a negative, since Tinta Negra Mole can make good if not great Madeira. I would suggest, though, that Madeira without at least 10 years of age is fundamentally uninteresting. With age, it's great.

80 Italy: red extroverts

I last left Florence in a thunderstorm. As the train pulled slowly out of the station, lightning forked angrily at the Arno, and a clap seemed to shake the heavy carriage on its rails. I looked up from my notebook. Outside two small, shabby railway buildings, where the workers clocked on, perhaps, or ate their mid-shift sandwiches, were a pair of vines. Their shoots and tendrils curled up and around coarse wire frames providing, in the middle of steel and oil, a little shade, a little green solace, a little purple fruit.

Italy is the world's most vine-friendly country. No garden and few olive groves are complete without a vine or two. Vines grow by lakes, by roads, by woods, by themselves; they cover the country from the high mountain terraces of its Alpine debut down to the sweltering encore of Pantelleria, nearer Tunisia than Sicily, where huge Muscat grapes loll on mats in the sunshine before being made into wines which smell and taste like marmalade. In no other country in the world do vines grow so ubiquitously. Everyone in Italy knows wine; everyone in Italy drinks wine. Like air, potatoes or the 18th of August, it's taken for granted.

In this fact lie both the strengths and failings of Italian wine. The strengths include diversity of climate and soil conditions, a huge library of grape varieties, a certain level of viticultural and winemaking proficiency, and the natural balance and complexity which some of Europe's longest winegrowing traditions deliver in the glass. Failings include the acceptance, sometimes, of second best being 'good enough'; a chaos of names facing consumers; and a wine law occasionally keener to preserve tradition for tradition's sake than to help consumers understand and enjoy the very best of Italian wine.

To explain all the flavours of Italy's hundreds of different red and white wines is barely possible in a weighty book, let alone in a few pages. Whenever I go to Italy, I come across wines and denominations I've never heard of – and I'm meant to know about these things. Nevertheless, north to south, there are a few key families of flavours which will help you get your bearings.

First of all, it's worth noting that wine in Italy

is, in principle, red. White wine takes the back seat, plays a submissive role, in all but a few regions – chiefly those of the Alps and the Adriatic coast. These vary from pungent, lemony and incisive to relatively delicate and understatedly floral. In general, though, more typical Italian whites throughout the entire country are clean, modestly fruity, cautiously characterful – good with all sorts of food or on their own, but not the kind of thing which will keep you awake at night rolling recalled flavours around your tongue. They've got names like Soave, Frascati, Orvieto, Albana or Verdicchio. There's plenty of room for such wines in the world. Just as philosophers enjoy watching football matches, models sometimes like to wear old jeans and baggy jumpers, and brain surgeons relish a game of darts, so the most fastidious tasters want a simple quaff once in a while.

Reds are an entirely different matter. Italy has what are the world's most energetic, extrovert, vivid, high-velocity and rousing reds. It's as if all the character which appears to have drained out of Italy's modest and unobtrusive whites has been collected in a big vat and poured into the reds. They take personality to what sometimes seems combative lengths.

The best known is Chianti, made from Sangiovese grapes: full of pungent, vibrant fruit which can remind you of plums, apples or raspberries, with subtle overtones of coffee and bay leaves. Unfortunately it's enormously variable, and the worst (of which there is much, often deceitfully admixed with wines of other regions) is depressingly thin and sour. Give cheap Chianti a wide berth.

Other wines made, in whole or in part, from the Sangiovese grape include Vino Nobile di Montepulciano, Carmignano, Pomino and, most impressively of all, Brunello di Montalcino. The slopes which tumble down from the typically Tuscan hilltop town of Montalcino are where, for me, Sangiovese reaches its apogee: dense, piercing, sometimes fiercely and aristocratically tannic, yet deeply if drily curranty, too, with a smoky, liquorice-like aftertaste which seems to last for minutes. Look out for its little brother, Rosso di Montalcino, to give you a taste of the same remarkable spot on earth for rather less outlay.

There are other, much lighter Sangiovese-based wines, too, such as Sangiovese di Romagna: jolly and juicy, boisterous and unsubtle, but unmatched for chasing down piles of pasta and then cleaning the oil and cheese from your gleaming lips.

Italy's other Big Red Name is Barolo – though, in fact, the area it comes from, Piedmont, is in some ways more significant in flavour terms than the top wine itself. Piedmont means 'foot of the mountain' (in French, but let's not get hung up on detail), and its reds have some of the craggy grandeur of the rocks which shake themselves skywards just beyond their vineyards. They're not easy; they're not soft; they're not juicy. Instead their excellence lies in an arresting diversity of flavour, wealth of tannin and amplitude of acidity. They're a challenge but, like most challenges, rewarding, too, unloading scents and flavours of plums, violets, roses, tar, leather and tobacco.

Nebbiolo, craggiest of all, is the variety which Barolo and Barbaresco are made from. Great Barolo seems to age as well as any wine on earth, holding itself intact for decades and slowly undergoing transformations that tend to suggest leather, game and the extraordinary white truffles nudged locally out of the earth by thin men with nimble dogs on misty autumn mornings. White truffles have no taste to speak of, but the smell ... One truffle beneath a glass dome can perfume an entire restaurant. They are said to mimic male pheromones. I'm not convinced about that, but there's certainly something penetratingly animal in the white truffle's scent, hovering excitingly on the border between decency and indecency, day and night, health and corruption. Something of this, too, in the maturer wines of the place: thus you may trace synergies between different gifts of one earth.

After Nebbiolo come Barbera and Dolcetto. These have the almost caustic fruit of Nebbiolo but lack its seven veils of tannin; Barbera, it's worth noting, can have even higher acidity. Dolcetto is meant to be (semantically speaking) 'the sweet one', but this is sweetness of a distinctly Piedmontese order. Just a certain rounded quality, in other words, to the brisk and piquant plum.

Great reds don't finish there. If you've been to Italy and enjoyed the nation's frankly bitter apéritifs (like Campari) and digestifs (like Ramazzotti or Averna), then you won't be surprised to know that Italy makes bitter-edged red wines, too. The great regional specialist in this kind of flavour is the Veneto: a region of dappled orchards and hills set inland from the murky lagoon. Valpolicella, in Verona's back yard, is the most famous name, but one often traduced and betrayed by appallingly thin and peevish wines. Seek out the best producers, look for a type of Valpolicella called Ripasso, or throw caution to the wind and buy a bottle of Amarone. This is strong, masterful, *da meditatizione* as they say locally ('for meditating over'), made from bunches of grapes that have been dried in racks before vinification. The cherry kernel and cherry characters of a good basic Valpolicella become, here, concentrated into something dense, drily rich, rose-perfumed and, yes, faintly bitter (*amaro* in Italian). Recioto is a sweeter and less alcoholic version.

The reds of southern Italy are different,

especially in terms of balance: the cut and thrust which you find in the wines of the north is replaced by something wider, fuller, sometimes softer, sometimes tangier. Those of Puglia (sold under various names, including Salice Salentino) tend to have a relaxed and raisiny sweetness to them, rather like Grenache-based Rhône wines – though the grape here is the Negroamaro. Montepulciano is another grape variety which can give pleasingly chewy, full-fruited reds (it's also used in the Marches for the worthy Rosso Cònero); and Aglianico can turn in eyebrow-raisingly good reds, too, in a muscular, forceful, earthy and extract-laden style (look out for Aglianico del Vulture and Taurasi).

Sicily and Sardinia, finally, are home to some fine reds, in the main made from Nero d'Avola (also called Calabrese) in Sicily and from Cannonau (our old friend Grenache) in Sardinia. The best are deep, sweet, sensibly oaked and articulate, though few in number: they're generally the top reds of private producers with international perspectives. Nine-tenths of the huge amount of wine produced, in particular, on Sicily is designed only to harvest European Union distillation subsidies. It's a pity, because both islands could produce wines to worry Chile, Australia or the South of France if they could overcome local corruption and inertia.

Anything else? How about a glass of Marsala to finish? This is a fine fortified wine which has more or less successfully committed suicide by selling all manner of sweet and sickly confections under its once-distinguished name. There is good stuff still to be found: it's dry, and the kind of words to look for are *vergine*, *secco*, *superiore* and *riserva*. It tastes like a smooth, crooning cousin of dry amontillado or oloroso sherry, with buttered almond richness of flavour.

81 Germany: the quivering embrace

It's a sunny summer afternoon. You're out on the water, whose glitter is cut from time to time by the determined and surprisingly swift advent of a bulky barge. On its cabin roof is perched, like a top hat on a wrestler, the bargee's bright new black Mercedes.

You lie back on your deck chair and look to each side of you. Mountainous shoulders of slate, dotted minutely with vines, ascend to tiny green shelves nestling beneath peaks of such inaccessibility that their vineyards have been abandoned and now sprawl moodily amid a tangle of grass. Occasionally a castle appears, sometimes ruined, always dramatic, its windows promising a fatal fall to any lover or lunatic leaning incautiously out of them. Birds glide past its turrets. It's hard not to hum a stately Wagnerian tune.

Germany's wineland is the second region I'd pick, after Portugal's Douro Valley, as being among the world's most memorably beautiful. I'm thinking of the Rhine Gorge between Koblenz and Mainz, but a boat trip down the smaller and more serpentine Mosel would be prettier still. Most of Germany's vineyards cling to rivers, steeply. The towns are old and half-timbered, bright with geraniums; winegrowers' wrought-iron signs compete with each other for intricacy; even an oom-pah band sounds appealing there. After a glass or two, anyway.

Ah yes, the wines. Unlike the landscape, the wines have no rivals at all; for better or worse, they're unique. Time, in other words, to re-tune our taste buds.

The most important thing to remember with German wine is that it is constructed in a completely different way to most other wines. Alcohol is no longer the point. The point, German growers would say, is to produce a wine which imitates the excitement of biting into a fresh grape: fruit acids and fruit sugars quivering in each other's spell, locked in an energetic embrace.

Regions and grape varieties, of course, make some difference. The Mosel, with its Saar and Ruwer tributaries, is where the lightest and finest of all Germany's wines come from; alcohol levels can often be as low as 7.5 or eight per cent there, thus barely perceptible within the filigree structure of fruity acidity trimmed with crystal sweetness. The volume grows a little louder in regions such as the Rheingau, Nahe, Rheinhessen and Rheinpfalz, though the premise is the same: fine balance combined with clarity and limpidity of fruit flavours (apple, grape, peach, nectarine, apricot: the list of the fruits such wines can suggest is almost endless). Mineral flavours, especially slate, are a vital part of Riesling's appeal in Germany's classic areas, too.

Franconia's wines offer something a little different: absolute dryness combined with alcohol levels on a par with international norms give whites which the severe continental climate seems to endow with an electrical crispness. Only in sunny Baden, facing Alsace across the Rhine, does German wine grow alcoholically fat and relaxed in any way whatsoever: here the wines are dry yet full and rounded, with light yet glycerous reds on offer in unusually large quantities for Germany.

In terms of grape varieties, Riesling is the name to look out for on almost all of the country's best bottles, especially from classic regions such as the Mosel and the Rheingau. There is, indeed, no other country in the world whose great wines are so closely identified with the style and flavours of a single grape. Germany's grandeur is Riesling, and Riesling's greatest performances are given on the rocky river slopes of its homeland.

There are, though, a large number of other

grape varieties grown in German vineyard regions, partly explained by the fact that the Germans are assiduous vine breeders; these varieties usually appear on the labels of German wines. To some extent, they resemble each other in style: many of the whites are more muskily, spicily or florally aromatic than fresh, pure, fruit-spun Riesling is, with softer and sometimes kitschier flavours on the palate (Bacchus, Huxelrebe, Morio-Muskat, Müller-Thurgau and Scheurebe all fall more or less into this category). Silvaner tends to be dry and earthy; Weissburgunder (Pinot Blanc) and Grauburgunder (Pinot Gris – also known as Ruländer if it's slightly sweet) are full, fresh, yet relatively neutral by comparison with examples from Alsace. Germany's best reds are light to mid-weight Pinot Noir (Spätburgunder); deeper if sharper reds may come from other varieties like Dornfelder or Lemberger.

A quantity of other verbiage piles up on German wine labels. 'Trocken' means dry; in fact, in Germany it tends to signify a very sharp, acid wine in most regions except Rheinpfalz and Baden. 'Halbtrocken' is semi-dry (and generally more palatable); if neither term appears on a label, assume the wine has some residual sugar. 'Kabinett', 'Spätlese', 'Auslese', 'Beerenauslese' and 'Trockenbeerenauslese' are all terms describing the amount of sugar in the grapes when they were picked; in practice, Kabinett tends to be a lightly fruity wine and Spätlese a more fully fruity wine, while the other three terms generally indicate a sweet, very sweet and intensely sweet wine respectively. 'Eiswein' is made by pressing grapes left to freeze on the vines in the depths of winter; this concentrates both sugar and acidity, and drinking a young Eiswein is the nearest you can get to sword-swallowing without metal becoming involved.

Occasionally, wines up to Auslese level are
made in Trocken or Halbtrocken styles, in which
case forget everything I told you about low alcohol:
Auslese Trocken wines from regions like Baden can
end up with more alcohol than Châteauneuf-du-
Pape! It's all on the label, anyway, so have a close
look before you toss back your goblet in one go.

The other piece of information you might like
to pursue on German labels is vineyard descriptions.
This brims with difficulties for the consumer, since
powerful German wine cooperatives have managed
to manipulate German wine law so that consumers
have no way of telling (without looking everything
up in reference books) whether a vineyard name
on a label describes a huge collection of vineyards
or a genuine single vineyard of historical tradition.
Germany, too, has no recognized vineyard classification
system as yet. But if you find great German wine to
your taste (and, I promise, there's simply nothing else
in the world like it), then vineyards count – so buy a
reference book or two to help you advance through the
thorny thicket of names.

How do you drink German wines? My own
preference is to enjoy them before a meal, as
apéritifs. Indeed, on a warm summer's evening I
don't think there is a better apéritif than a choice,
intricate, finely woven Spätlese from the Mosel,
Nahe or Rheingau. It rouses and freshens the mouth,
teases the senses, engages and relaxes the mind
without befuddling it and quenches thirst as few
wines can.

Oh, one final thing. Liebfraumilch. Cheap
German wines can, despite their utterly tarnished
reputation, be pleasant, off-dry quaffers; they can
also be nasty and sickly. Either way, though, they are
always simple in flavour, so if you want to taste what
German wines really can and should be, look a little
further than Lieb.

82
England: sparkling hopes

I'm looking out of the window. It's late May, in Kent
– one of England's key winegrowing counties. We've
had some generous weather recently: hot, sunny
days; cool, misty nights. Today is grey, though, and
chilly. I've just been to the post office; I wore a
jacket. Sunglasses were unnecessary.

What would the weather be like today in the
Loire valley, in Champagne, in Alsace? It might be
cloudy, too, of course, but even if it was, somehow I
doubt I would have needed my jacket, and the
brightness falling from the clouds would probably
mean I'd have been just a little more comfortable
with my sunglasses on. England, you see, is the
grapevine's most northern outpost: the one with the
weakest light, the most inconstant sunshine, the most
tentative heat. There are just a couple of spots in
Germany – Saale-Unstrut near Leipzig and Sachsen,
near the Czech border – which lie as far north,
making wine thanks to sheltered river valleys.
Viticulture in England is possible because of the sea
which surrounds the country, moderating the climate
to a far greater extent than people living on the same
latitude as Warsaw or Minsk have any right to
expect.

You need patience to be an English
winegrower. Everything's late, uncertain, touch and
go. But when it works, the results can be ...

Imagine a wine not so much white as silver,
with breeze-clean aromas of fresh green fruits and
hedgerow flowers. Lots of acidity, sure, but it's ripe
and rounded, not thin and pinched, allowing the
wine's apple, lemon and grape flavours to gallop
through the mouth, leaving a refreshing fruit surf to
subside in their wake. That's the English ideal,
though it needs a good summer to realise it. Wines
(or summers) which fall short of the ideal tend to

produce thinner, sharper, more plainly acidulous wines – or wines given a heavy dose of concentrated grape juice to balance them out.

The great hope for English viticulture is sparkling wine. It began to dawn on growers a year or two ago that England's downland vineyards were part of exactly the same chalk formation as Champagne's rolling, white-soiled hills. High-acid base wines, too, are part of the Champagne formula – and England can certainly produce those without great effort. Sure enough, early attempts to produce top-quality sparkling wine in England have managed to create blends of great crispness, precision and depth. The real problem so far is that the grape varieties which most readily provide satisfactory ripeness in England aren't the trio hallowed by Champagne tradition, namely Chardonnay, Pinot Noir and Pinot Meunier. The flavours, in other words, lack the purity and breed of Champagne – so far. Experience may improve matters. At least one producer, in any case, has proved that Champagne varieties for sparkling wine are viable in England.

83
Eastern Europe: renovations in progress

Politics and wine, you might think, don't mix. You'd be wrong. Wine is agriculture, and agriculture, particularly in developing countries, is never far from the political heart of a nation.

When I nosed around Bulgaria's vineyards in mid 1997 I became all too aware of this. Bulgarians working in the wineries are eager to build on their export success over the previous two decades. The country's sluggish approach to land reform, though, means that the vineyards are falling into slow disrepair, like houses on which the paintwork is peeling and from which the roof tiles are gently sliding. You can't make good wine from bad grapes. So the taste of Bulgarian red wine, too – once so softly and soothingly currant y, so round, warm and stewy – is now becoming thinner, greener and more herbaceous. You can taste, in other words, the fact that the vines are badly pruned, the foliage unkempt, the bunches meagre and shaded. Bulgarian wine is slowly losing touch with much of its opposition, though it remains highly competitive on price. White wine-making, to be fair, is improving, with crisper unwooded wines and a subtler use of oak on those which have spent some time in new barrels.

When Bulgaria finally gets its vineyards into shape, there will be no reason why it shouldn't reacquire some of the prominence it once enjoyed as what one might now call 'the Chile of Europe'. Much of the country is ideal vineyard terrain; the climate is relatively reliable; winemaking competent and wine itself culturally familiar. Politics, though, come first.

Romania, too, is finding the move forward a slow one, though this is due above all to the position (two dozen kilometres behind everyone else) from which it began. Yet the prospects look good: Romania not only had famous historical wines of the kind which Bulgaria lacked (such as the sweet fat white Cotnari, made on the border with Moldova), but it also has areas which seem particularly well suited to certain grape varieties. The Burgundy-like hillsides of the Dealul Mare area, for example, make finely balanced, sweet-fruited Pinot Noir, as well as accessible Cabernets and Merlots and the supple dessert wine Tamaîîoasa. For the time being, assume that the taste of Romania, for both red and white wine, will be soft, smooth and easy-going; the future may bring deeper and more serious wines.

At present, Eastern Europe's most exciting wines come from Hungary. These divide into two distinct groups: Tokaji and everything else.

Tokaji was, in times past, a wine-producing area ranking in importance with Bordeaux, Burgundy or the Rhinelands. It's a picturesque region of volcanic hills, lying in the north-east of the country, near the border with Ukraine. After the political metamorphosis of 1989, foreign investment was welcomed – with the result that many of the best estates in Tokaji were hoovered up by western (particularly French) interests, and joint-venture companies created. In taste terms, what this meant was that the sweet (as well as the less widely exported dry, 'szamorodni') wines of Tokaji changed stylistically from the profile consumers had become used to over the previous two decades. They had always been intense and well balanced, with apple, autumn leaf and apricot flavours, but in the past they were both heavily oxidised (giving them a sherry-like tang) and pasteurised, giving them a plodding monotony. Modern, classic Tokaji is much less heavily oxidised, so that its tang is fugitive, merely there to stroke in extra complexity, and without pasteurisation its flavours are much fresher and more succulent, like freshly baked fruit pastries. The characteristic bitter edge of botrytis, too, is more palpable than in the past. Grandeur has returned to Tokaji. So, alas, have high prices.

The best of 'everything else' is accounted for by generally inexpensive, well made white wines and rather less satisfactory, sometimes rather slender, reds. My favourite Hungarian whites are those made from the fine indigenous grape varieties Furmint and Hárslevelü (both, incidentally, used for Tokaji): these are thick-textured, chewy, and subtly aromatic, suggesting limeflower, mint and pastry dough. Furmint has the higher acid levels of the two.

Unfortunately, these names are not seen as an asset on supermarket shelves around the rest of the world, so international varietals (Sauvignon Blanc, Pinot Blanc, Chardonnay & Co.) are now far more common. They can be aromatic, finely balanced and memorable, despite what I hope is a passing fad for picking the grapes barely ripe for extra 'crispness' (after a glass or two, drinkers push the bottle aside to nurse their acheing teeth and salivary glands). One Hungarian crossing which seems to have survived the onslaught of internationalisation is Irsai Oliver, a kind of crisped-up, stripped-back Gewürztraminer, full of musky scent.

Hungarian reds (despite their macho 'Bull's Blood' image) tend to be relatively light and slender. Generally, those from Bulgaria or Romania offer better value and more satisfactory balance.

Other East European wines are either good in quality but relatively uncommon on most export markets (such as the full and fruity white wines of Slovenia, the Czech Republic and Slovakia, many of them almost Alsace-like at best) or potentially good in quality but prevented from reaching that potential by lack of development or political turmoil (the wines of the former Yugoslavia, especially the robust reds of coastal Croatia and Montenegro, and those of former Soviet Republics like Georgia and Moldova). All I suggest you do is what I'll be doing: trying anything interesting which comes along.

84 USA and Canada: big time

North America is the home of the can-do culture. The American dream often signifies, in practical terms, the assertion of individual will over collective wisdom – and the determination to sell what results to someone else afterwards for a juicy profit. How do these things affect the wine scene?

First, wine gets made all over the continent, from Texas to British Columbia. If it is climatologically possible to ripen grapes, then someone (generally someone who's already made a fortune in machine couplings, novelty licence plates or chocolate chip cookies) will dream the activity into being. Since there are handsome fortunes aplenty in America, the results can be surprisingly good.

Winemaking on a large scale, though, only happens where viticulture is not only possible but advisable. Overwhelmingly, this means California, with Washington and Oregon also justifying their winegrowing with compelling bottles.

On the East Coast, there has been a tradition of making wines with vines which don't belong to the European *Vitis vinifera* vine family; these American vines or hybrids tend to give very simple, confectionery-like flavours. *Vinifera* vines are increasingly used, and up-and-coming areas like Long Island and Virginia can produce wines, both red and white, with a startling wealth and depth of flavour very much at odds with the snow-driven East Coast image. The last, southerly outreaches of Ontario are where most Canadian production is concentrated: vivid, palate-slicing ice wine (dessert wine made from the pressed juice of frozen grapes, in which sugars, acids and other elements are concentrated) is the headline-grabber, but Chardonnay and even Merlot can do well there in a restrained idiom.

The vast bulk of American's wine, though, comes from the west coast. "In the States, no one knows what anything's supposed to taste like." Philosophical winegrower Randall Grahm points out, here, perhaps the greatest handicap facing those making wine in America: public taste. The can-do culture and the American dream, translated into culinary terms and cut adrift from the base of a long and local agricultural tradition, often decays into a nightmare. I've been served sweet 'muffins' with broccoli quiche before now in America; the quality of bread (as accurate a measurement as any of a nation's ability to eat well) is, state to state, uniformly grim; most food items sold in American supermarkets are loaded with sugar. America has polished, expensive restaurants and great chefs, but the ordinary roadside and supermarket food is the worst in the developed world.

The American wine scene reflects this division faithfully. If you're rich, you can drink great wines; if you're not, you drink mush. California is producing some of the finest non-European wines of the century – in tiny quantities, for sale in those expensive restaurants or through mail-order lists for which there is in turn a waiting list. The best Californian red wines have great density of flavour without hardness or toughness; the best whites a striking silky lushness. Climate – California's golden haze – is at the root of these characteristics. Here's Randall Grahm again. "The real strength of California is its climate: we just have benign weather. Our soils aren't so good, but our climate gives that lush, soft palate impression. It gives a very different tannic structure to European wines. We get softer tannins, which is the result of the length of our growing season. Europeans would kill for that. Well maybe not kill, but maim for sure." Winemaking, too, from individuals in the Californian vanguard, is superb: thoughtful, intuitive, site-sensitive, taking the very best of the European tradition and reworking it in another environment altogether.

Most of the Californian wines you or I are likely to encounter, though, come from much bigger producers; here the standard varies greatly. Their problem is a massive stylistic uncertainty. Should they be sweet, because American consumers expect everything to be sweet? Should they be oaky, because American consumers can click on to that? Should they be light, dark, alcoholic, less alcoholic, with or without malolactic, with or without other varietal admixtures, with or without a little back-blended grape juice? And what's the grape variety in fashion this year anyway? The end result tends to be a hovering somewhere in the middle, a hesitant blandness – and sometimes (as in the case of 'Blush' Zinfandel, a sweet and flaccid rosé) something downright repellent. Of course, there are exceptions, particularly among larger producers with a securely regional vineyard base; California's warmth, generosity and amplitude (it's the home of the hunk, after all) slides out unapologetically into the light in their wines.

Washington and Oregon are both working through their adolescence in wine terms at present, though the nature of their internal conflicts is different. Washington thought (because of its severely continental climate and icy winters) that it ought to be America's Rhineland, whereas the last few years have shown that dark, sappy, vigorous reds from varieties like Cabernet Sauvignon and Merlot are in fact most successful in the sun-roasted, desert vineyards of this eerie moonscape, cut only by roads, starlight and mighty rushing rivers. Oregon, which looks more like America's Cotswolds, chose from the start a burgundian trajectory for itself, with Pinot Noir and Chardonnay in the cockpit; success hasn't been as uniform or as easy as everyone hoped, and, of late, an Alsace ideal of Pinot Gris has begun to supplant Chardonnay. Nonetheless, its Pacific Burgundy project is broadly on course, though, for great wines, a rare combination of inspired winemaking and a good summer is needed. Neither

Oregon nor Washington are geared to produce inexpensive wine, which is why neither state as yet figures widely on export markets.

85 Chile: the natural

What is it, I wonder, that you've most wanted to do in your life? Write a publishable novel, maybe; play a sport or a musical instrument outstandingly well; or perhaps simply be the best in your field at your job? Whatever it is, you've probably achieved, by great efforts, some palpable success – then along breezes some naturally gifted yet otherwise unimpressive newcomer who immediately eclipses, with little apparent effort, your own attainments. It's galling or worse, I know.

In wine terms, that's Chile. No other country on earth is so naturally well endowed for making lovely (yes, lovely) red wine. Central Chile (since it's important to be specific about this one-nation geography encyclopedia, which begins with the driest desert in the world and ends in miserable, sun-forsaken Patagonia) is the kind of place where a walking stick left stuck in the ground for half-an-hour will begin to sprout leaves. Want to make decent inexpensive red Cabernet Sauvignon? In Chile, you have to try quite hard to spoil it in any way whatsoever. And with a little effort, you can make wines that merit, more than any others anywhere in the world, that adjective 'lovely': brim-full of pure fruit, with supple tannins and moderate acids giving a rounded, supple, juicy sheen. Above all, they have drinkability: you want nothing more after one glass than another of exactly the same thing. This, as it happens, is rather unusual with many non-European wines; it's more typical for them to impress enormously at first sip but to catch in the throat on the second glass. That's why Chile has rival wine-producing countries, from France to the Antipodes, worried.

Chilean white wines have less natural grace and less effortless poise than do the reds, and the climate in most of its winegrowing regions (the cooler Casablanca valley aside) is not naturally propitious for whites. Chilean winemaking upgrades over the last few years, though, has improved the whites markedly; they don't have the natural zest and zing of New Zealand or the Loire valley, but they do have a kind of comfortable, creamy plumpness to them, with subtly oaked Chardonnay proving particularly successful. At the moment, if you were to ask me to recommend an inexpensive, uncomplicated red or white wine, I would unhesitatingly direct you towards Chile.

But what if you wanted something a little more complicated? Something with genuine regional character? Something with an extractive density behind its sweet, supple fruit? This is the great challenge for Chile, and most producers there are now wheeling out sententiously priced 'top wines' with which they hope to conquer the world. As yet, all they are really doing is amplifying Chile's basic gifts of delicious, pure fruit – which is unsurprising, considering the siting and management of most Chilean vineyards. I am convinced that Chile will one day make very great wines, but only after a lot more site research and viticultural work. In this respect, those natural gifts of Chile may hold the country back: why struggle with the uncertainties and tiresome economics of great wine, when you can make good wine so easily and so profitably? Let's hope, though, that the Chileans have more ambition than that, and that the country doesn't rest on the laurels which aptitude has already brought it.

86 Argentina: the shy monster

Argentina's wines seem, at first glance, as if they ought to be a mirror-image of Chile's. They occupy more or less the same latitude and, as the condor flies, are not even very far apart (a couple of hundred aerial kilometres separates Santiago and Mendoza). All that divides them is a lofty, mirage-like, snow-capped mountain range: the Andes.

All? It'll take you seven hours to drive over, and you'll need several generous brandies afterwards.

Open a few bottles of wine, too, and you'll see that Argentina's wines are very definitely different from Chile's. The inexpensive ones are perhaps coarser, deeper, more thumpingly flavourful, with the reds often being made from grape varieties uncommon in Chile, like Malbec or Tempranillo (labelled Tempranilla in Argentina). More expensive reds, too, lack Chile's lyrical, soaring, pure fruit style; they're tighter-grained, earthier, more complex and (from traditional producers rather than the California-influenced New Wave) more European in style. Whites vary from relatively fat and oily versions of the classic international varieties to fragrant, crispish wines from a variety called Torrontés (which might or might not have come from Spanish Galicia).

Argentina is in an export honeymoon period at present: a profusion of bargains from this shy monster (it produces around twice as much wine as Chile) are fetching up on shop shelves around the world. Experience from exporters like New Zealand, Australia and Chile itself suggests that this will not last. Once Argentina has fought its way to export success, it will want a fair price for its wine – so make the most of the situation now.

87 South Africa: slow fusion

Bright light, to begin with, saturates the shadowless landscape before you and lends the green of the vineyards and the reds and yellows of the flowers an almost violent depth. The clear air abolishes distance. Abrupt mountains loom; on their toothy edges carpets of cloud teeter without ever quite tumbling over the edge. The graceful scrolling on the gable facades of 300-year-old white houses redraws itself tremblingly in calm dam waters; a dozen Guernsey cows are being herded home by a lithe black figure. Here it is, then: the third in my personal triumvirate of exceptionally beautiful vineyard areas. Welcome to the Cape.

Perhaps it's the distracting beauty of the place, perhaps it's the troubled burden of history, or perhaps it's the peculiar cultural mix inspiring its winemakers, but South Africa is taking a while to find its own identity within the community of wine nations. That beauty is not chimerical: the Cape is an exceptionally propitious area to grow wine grapes. Yet history means that most of the vineyards are planted with white grape varieties meant for brandy production, and history also means that many of the classic red grape varieties planted in South Africa's vineyards are virus-affected, and thus perform less well than they should. History means that those who make wines do not necessarily know and understand their vineyards intimately; that's the work of their many quiet labourers. In cultural terms, there has been a reverence within South Africa for the tough, bruising and aggressive red, on the basis that such wines 'age well' and are 'European' in style; some South African winemakers like to see themselves as the Europeans of the New World. Alas, though, an ugly young wine only ever turns into an ugly old one. More recently, clumsily oaked whites have been a hazard.

It is, though, slowly fusing, slowly coming together. As it happens, those white varieties planted for brandy production have carved out for South Africa a useful niche in export markets. With skilful winemaking, they produce fresh, fruity, boisterous and well balanced white wines offering a price/quality ratio no other New World country can even approach.

Pinotage is another ace: this locally achieved crossing of Pinot Noir and Cinsault is sometimes a little rasping and rubbery, but, increasingly, producers are using it to create reds whose plummy fruit has sweet depth and rich, supple tannins. Unlike America's Zinfandel, even relatively inexpensive and unambitious examples retain their personality.

Like Australia, South Africa is beginning to discover regionality. Sometimes, as with the fragrant, precisely structured whites of the Constantia region, this is due to climate; sometimes, as with the creamy, almost unctuous Chardonnays produced in the limestone-rich Robertson valley, soils are a more important contributory factor.

Then there are the general, estate-to-estate improvements in both viticulture and winemaking. There are still dull, clumsy, and unattractive wines exported from South Africa, but the best are acquiring a depth, pungency and brightness of definition which sets the country apart from its New World rivals. Unlike those rivals, too, South Africa seems equally well equipped to produce both red and white wines – though, if present trends continue, it will be reds which the world wants more of in the end.

88 New Zealand: the vivid south

Now here's a country which the whole wine world envies. Other New-World wine-producers are jealous because it's the only one in their club with a natural and effortless white-wine vocation, and one of the few, too, to present the consumer with an instantly world-beating regional/varietal style, in Marlborough Sauvignon Blanc. Old-World producers turn grape-green because New Zealand's wines – made from almost brand-new, low-cost, highly mechanised vineyards – command a higher average price on many export markets than do the wines of their own labour-intensive, anciently planted, historically famous vineyards. And consumers?

Actually, consumers are in danger of being left out of the equation at the moment. New Zealand's wines have been such a success that there simply aren't enough of them to go around, and prices are consequently so high that they are beginning to look like poor value for money. You might try one for a treat, understand what all the fuss was about, but quietly decide that nonetheless you can live quite happily with only the occasional fix of that ..., that ...

Well, what is it exactly? Sauvignon Blanc is the country's defining grape variety: its wine seems to quiver in the glass, exhaling green and leafy scent, like a breeze darting about woods and hedgerows at a midsummer dusk. It slices through the mouth with some of the quicksilver rapidity of a Loire valley white wine, yet there's usually a much richer texture there, with more fruit upholstery – green fruits like gooseberries and limes, with some asparagus richness, too. On occasion, there's also a monotony, an over-simple sherbetty quality.

Marlborough is the region which produces this sort of wine most regularly, yet good Sauvignon from other areas, like Hawkes Bay and Gisborne, can pull it off, too. Chardonnay, Riesling, Chenin Blanc and even Gewürztraminer all produce exciting wines in New Zealand, built on that same vein of rich yet vivid, lushly acidic fruit; Semillon makes less sense, and Müller-Thurgau (once the country's most widely planted grape variety) is now waving goodbye, though you'll still taste it in blends which don't specify their grape variety.

Reds are more problematic. Ripe, bright Cabernet, Merlot and Cabernet Franc (and mixtures thereof) are possible, though not in every vineyard and not in every vintage; there are plenty of herbaceous, unripe and unappealing failures pushing the price of the few successes to eyebrow-raising levels. Pinot Noir is a much better bet for New Zealand; indeed, the best of these are superb, rivalling California's greatest Pinots as out-and-out Burgundy beaters. They retain New Zealand's hallmark vividness, yet lap up classy oak to make full and balanced wines of powerful depth and resonant fruit. Martinborough is the key region here, though Marlborough is also promising; prices, once again, are balloon-high.

Sparkling wines, finally, make New Zealand's final claim on our attention and our credit cards, and as usual they do it plausibly enough. It's a question of taste as to how much fruit flavour you think appropriate in sparkling wine; Champagne, in fact, does not have a great deal, whereas New Zealand's sparkling wines tend to have more. They also have natural incision and 'cut' without, crucially, the producer having to pick the grapes too early, which is why their place in the forefront of New World sparkling wines seems assured.

89
Australia: the challenge of the soil

I've been cold in Australia. It wasn't even winter, either, just early autumn, up in the Adelaide Hills, on a cloudy afternoon sitting outside one of the most appealingly sited houses I've ever visited – the home of Chris Laurie of Hillstowe. Modern and glassy, it occupies one end of a duck-busy dam in a hollow at the bottom of deep stringybark tree woods. The dipping, plunging, roller-coaster vineyards of Hillstowe are cut into the same woods, gathering sometimes shy sunlight by the same positional strategems as any vineyard in Alsace or Burgundy. Thus we sat, in coats for warmth, sipping wine and watching red-browed finches perch in a line on a small wire fence, lured into proximity by seeds on a bird-table, while all about us the soft yodelling of the Australian magpie fell echoingly down through the woods, resembling a wind-chime struck under water.

I'm telling you this partly for the pleasure of recalling a beautiful scene, but partly to point out that not all of Australia's vineyards are sited in the furnace of the outback, irrigated into being by workers whose biggest health risk is not alcoholism but skin cancer. In temperature terms, many of Australia's classic regions (Coonawarra, the Eden valley, the Yarra valley) are no warmer than Bordeaux, Tuscany or the northern Rhône valley. Others, of course, are warmer. The advantage that most have is that weather conditions are generally more predictable than in Europe, without the same risk of rain at the wrong moment.

Australians are beginning to pay more attention to regional differences between areas at present, and soil factors, too, receive more attention that they used to. There is a great deal of potential variety in Australia, partly accounted for by the huge distances between its vineyard areas. Impose a map of Australia over one of Europe and you find that the vineyards of Margaret River in Western Australia would lie near Madrid while those of the Hunter Valley would be in the Black Sea.

Yet the success of Australian wine has in some ways been built on ignoring or even burying those differences between the intrinsic character of the raw materials; it's been a product of winemaking skills above all, and of a distinctive winemaking philosophy. "We've come up in general," says Stephen Henschke, one of Australia's finest winemakers, "with wines which express flavours of the fruits, not of the earth or whatever, and that's been very appealing to people." It is this which has created big, bright flavours; it is this which has created the consistency and value with which Australia is synonymous on many export markets; it is this which means that, right across the wine spectrum from sparkling wines to massive reds and fortifieds, Australia has something of interest to offer.

Australians are, for the time being, undecided about how they want to build on that success. What will consumers want in the future? More consistent, reliable, fruity yet possibly monotonous and uniform winemaker-dominated wines? Or a taste of the ancient continent itself, its salty red earth, its oxidised minerals, its gum-laden breezes, its multi-millennial thunder: genuine aboriginal wines?

For the time being, you just get glimpses of the latter through the square specs of the former. What might Australian red wine – and few would disagree that reds are what Australia in general is best suited to producing – taste like without all the winemaking stratagems which overlie it? "The flavour is broad, earthy and humid. There is little acidic tang but in its place a gripping sensation of mixed tannic and ferruginous qualities." That was one W. S. Benwell, writing about the taste of Bailey's Shiraz in a book published in 1960.

No longer. Modern-day big-blend Australian Shiraz has considerable 'acidic tang', most of which comes out of a sack; the tannins will be soft rather than 'gripping' and quite possibly added in powdered form; 'ferruginous qualities' will be held in check, since 'ferruginous qualities' don't win medals at wine shows. There will be a sweet overlay of American oak, perhaps derived from real barrels but just as likely shaken as oak chips over the fruit, or obtained by dunking wooded staves in the wine as it sits in steel vats. It's a great drink, but is it wine? And does it taste of Australia?

For many (and probably the majority of) consumers, the answer would be 'yes', since those are the kind of flavours they associate with Australia – hence the producers' dilemma. What tends to happen at present is that many smaller Australian winegrowers are taking more sensitive and restrained approaches to winemaking, in order to let the taste of their soils, their climate and the fruit flavours of a particular location come forward. Most of the larger producers which dominate Australian wine exports, though, continue to make 'winemaker' wines with formulaic levels of added acid, adjusted tannin and wood input – though in their more expensive wines, of course, the fruit quality is often outstanding, meaning that these adjustments and interventions are less starkly evident. Such wines are invariably impressive to taste – but sometimes difficult to drink. After a while, that obtruding acid catches in the throat, and the wine's lack of subtlety is likely to become more glaringly evident in the third glass than it was in the first.

Perhaps in the end the market will have the last say. Australian wine has proved so popular over the last decade that prices have risen fast. This means that Australia is now competing with France rather than Bulgaria, and having to please consumers who are able to buy and appreciate Europe's classic wines, rather than those who just want sound, inexpensive wine from any source. Those consumers may no longer be happy with the 'flavours of the fruits' alone; they want complexity, regional style and wines which taste of vineyards rather than winemaking.

90 Everything else: prizes and surprises

There's a lot of land lying between 20° and 50° in the northern hemisphere; much less disturbs the vast blue of the southern hemisphere. Potentially, any of that land might be suitable for vine-growing and wine-making: these are the world's two temperate zones, lands of four seasons, of cool, damp winters and warm, dry summers.

Sure enough, most of the tangential winegrowing areas not already covered in our hectic round-the-world tour lie in the northern hemisphere. Tangential? This is meant in the sense that exports from such regions to the key world wine-markets, like Britain or America, are not of major significance. (If you live in the former Soviet republic of Georgia, of course, your local wine supply will not be tangential but crucial.)

Austria
Imagine Germany with more warmth: that's lowland (Eastern) Austria. Its wines correspond to this profile, too: whites based on aromatic grape varieties, like Riesling, which have more alcohol and flesh than Germany's; solid, quaffing whites from the national grape, Grüner Veltliner; impressively lively versions of international hits such as Chardonnay; rich and

attractively priced dessert wines from the
Neusiedlersee, the biggest puddle in the world,
which Austria shares with Hungary and where noble
rot is rampant most autumns; and reds with enough
depth and substance to plunge any blind taster,
attempting to guess their origin, into despair. In
other words, it's a fascinating country for wine
lovers to explore. Safe, too: standards are high.

Switzerland

Sound wines sold under a confusing variety of names
at what, for those without Swiss bank accounts, seem
hilariously high prices. The whites are fresh, but
fuller in flavour than you'd imagine; the reds tend to
be soft, smooth, sometimes perfumed.

Greece, Cyprus and Turkey

Of these three countries, Greece is by far the most
interesting at present for the curious wine-drinker;
indeed, writing as one who loves this country of
stone, light, water and history, I believe Greece's
best wines are much underrated. These are its
Northern reds, especially Naoussa and Goumenissa
(Boutari is the most reliable producer for both):
chiselled and stony in flavour, somehow, but
reverberative and profound, the very opposite of
the mindlessly fruity New World wine-product, and
hence close to the heart of Europe's wine culture.
There are other good reds, too: Nemea on occasion,
and then a creditable crop of international varietals
and blends from ambitious private producers with
chic boutique wineries.

My favourite Greek white wine is retsina (from
Kourtakis) – served not too cold, in a waterside
taverna, from a half-litre bottle with a crown cap,
poured into little glass tumblers on a rickety table
whose throwaway paper tablecloth is clipped to its
edges. Retsina is a dull, though clean and well made,

white wine which is rendered interesting by the addition of resin from the Aleppo pine tree. The resin, like mint, has a pseudo-cooling effect on the tongue; the wine seems to taste of Greece's beautifully warm, dry and scented pine forests.

If you don't like retsina, the country has plenty of other whites to offer, including impressive (though expensive) Chardonnays. There are fine sweet Muscat wines, too, from Samos. The Peloponnese red sweet fortified wine Mavrodaphne is also well worth a try.

Cyprus has been struggling for years to escape from its past of imitation sherry and exports of mediocre wine to the Soviet Union; it has not yet done so. Even its great classic Commanderia, brown and sweet, is not what it once was.

Turkey has 1.5 million acres of vineyards. It produces fine table grapes and raisins but indifferent wines.

Israel and Lebanon
The Golan Heights, taken by Israel from Syria in 1967, and Lebanon's high Bekaa Valley are both fine places to produce wine – as Israel's Golan Heights Winery (selling under the Yarden and Gamla labels) and Lebanon's Château Musar and Kefraya have shown. Their red wines have a natural amplitude and sweetness and, as Musar demonstrates so memorably, a remarkable ability to age.

All of Lebanon's winegrowing is in the Bekaa. Israel also has vineyards in its lower, hotter coastal regions (Samson and Shomron); wines from here are much less impressive than from the Golan. Kosher vinification strictures also make good wine more difficult to produce than it might otherwise be – though not impossible, as the excellent Golan Heights winemaking team has shown.

The Former Soviet Union

Moldova, Georgia and the Crimea (in the Ukraine) are all areas with long winemaking traditions and often a fascinating patrimony of grape varieties – but they remain far adrift in terms of technology. When improvements come, the results should be exciting.

Mexico, Brazil, Peru, Uruguay

Mexico's Baja California can produce some firm and chunky reds, and Uruguay, too, can produce impressive wine, with Tannat the local speciality but international white varietals like Chardonnay also performing well. Peru's wines show less promise, and I have yet to taste any wine from Brazil's surprisingly large wine industry which is competitive, other than as a novelty, on international markets.

91 Vintage wine isn't always good wine

What's a vintage? Simple: it's a year.

I'm sure you've had, in your life, good years and bad years. So do vines. Your bad years may have been caused by unhappy school experiences, the loss of a job, the trauma of a divorce or the pain of illness. Bad years for vines are generally the consequence of ill-luck of a more meteorological kind: too much wind at flowering, too much rain just before harvest or, not inconceivably, too much sun and heat during high summer.

You kept going and pulled through; so, of course, do the vines. What's happened to you, nonetheless, marks you and changes you: grey hairs and facial lines outside; defensiveness, caution and fatigue within. What's happened to the vines, likewise, conditions the composition of their grapes
— and the wine made from them.

You could view a vine as an extraordinarily sensitive measuring device for weather conditions, with drinkers tasting the results rather than technicians reading them from a roll of graph paper. Good vintages taste great; bad vintages taste lousy. Winemakers try to ensure that bad vintages taste as good as they can; this, paradoxically, is why many of them are actually more proud of their lesser wines (for which they worked very hard) than their great ones (for which they merely stood back and let nature take its course). Nevertheless, even the greatest winemaker on earth can't cheat nature, which is why it's worth learning as much about vintages as you can from newspaper reports and wine reference books.

There is, as usual, a qualification to make. The sunnier and warmer a wine-growing region, the less vintages matter. The reason why no one ever talks about good years or bad years for retsina is that vintages don't make a drachma's worth of difference to this wine. Year in and year out, the white Savatiano grapes which are used for retsina get reliably ripe long before there's any sign of rain over Attica; they are picked and vinified in the same way as the previous year, with the addition of the same amount of Aleppo pine resin; and the wine tastes just as good (or as bad, depending on your point of view) as last year. The same is true of large tracts of wine-producing southern Europe, California, Chile, Argentina and South Africa. It's only as you travel further north in the northern hemisphere, or further south in the southern hemisphere, that vintage differences become clearly apparent.

The pity of it is that most of the world's greatest wines, in both hemispheres, come from areas where vintages are variable or very variable. Let no one ever tell you that vintage differences are 'overstated' from Bordeaux, Burgundy, Tuscany, Piedmont or the northern Rhône valley, just to name a few key regions. Wine from these areas after poor vintages are profoundly disappointing, whereas those tricky conditions seem, when everything goes well, to produce more complex and rewarding wines than a simpler, hotter, sunnier, plainer season.

Finally, you may come across wines with no vintage date on them. Champagne is the best known example, but this will also include many ports, sherries and some ordinary wines, too. There's nothing dubious or suspicious about this: the producer is either telling you he's blended together the wines of a number of different vintages (as in Champagne: a sensible idea, since the deficiencies of one year can be remedied by the strengths of another); that the vintage is of no consequence; or indeed that the blending process creates something better than individual years can ever do.

Indeed you may sometimes see, on the back labels of bottles of sherry, reference to something called 'the solera system'. This constitutes a small hill of well filled casks: each new vintage that comes along is emptied, to a greater or lesser degree, into all the casks, blending as it does so with larger or smaller amounts of many previous vintages. In this way, the concept of vintage is utterly annihilated, and simple new wine is always given the stiffening gravity and complexity of old. The wine drawn off at the end of the system, too, is consistent from year to year – as will be the brand of sherry which you buy.

92 Look for the producer's name

Remember, from back in section 49, the four avenues by which you could, theoretically, manage to know everything there was to know about wine? The first avenue was grape varieties; the second regions. In the last section, we discussed the importance of the third avenue: vintages. Here, finally, is the fourth: the producers themselves.

One of the most attractive aspects of wine is the way in which it defeats conglomerates, multinationals and large companies of all sorts. There will never be a Coca-Cola of wine; there will never be a McDonalds of wine; there will never be a Ford, or BMW, or even Alfa-Romeo of wine. Wine grapes are an agricultural product, produced by hundreds of thousands of farmers around the world, many of whom actually make and sell their wine themselves. They, as much as their vineyards, are the guarantors of the very first of wine's qualities: its diversity.

Of course, there are large companies involved in wine production; the global elephant is the American producer Gallo. Chile has Concha y Toro; Australia has Penfold's, Hardy's, Lindeman's and others; New Zealand is dominated by Montana. In general, European wine production is less a fiefdom of large producers: its wine laws, indeed, are a way of ensuring that small producers enjoy the sort of access to domestic and foreign markets that, under the most rigorous free-market conditions, only large producers can afford.

Most large producers create good and occasionally great wines, but the vast bulk of their production is ordinary, sound wine of little marked character or individuality. The most interesting wines, in America as much as in France or Italy, tend to be those produced by smaller producers. The overwhelming majority of great wines, too, are the work of individuals. And what does that mean?

Names – thousands of them. I'm sorry: that's the way it is. Providing those names is beyond the scope of this book: that's the job of some of the books

I suggest you move on to in 'Further Reading'.

Before we leave the subject, though, perhaps I could stress the importance of individuals and why it's worth putting effort into learning a few of their names. It's no exaggeration to say that, in any given region, the top producer's wine will be perhaps eight or ten times as good as the worst producer's. That's a great deal more pleasure. Sometimes you'll have to pay commensurately more, but not always. Certainly, if you're buying wine in case quantities, you should either try to taste a bottle first for yourself – or follow the most trustworthy of recommendations. Which brings us to the next subject.

93 Recommendations: use with caution

My trade is treachery. Well, not exactly: perhaps treacherous is a better word. Like all wine journalists, I'm a peddler of recommendations. Wine is confusing and chaotic, so suggestions matter. And they can be treacherous.

I don't mean by this that the wines I recommend may prove disappointing. I'm sure this happens, of course: all beauty is subjectively appreciated, and none more so than beauty of scent and flavour. Your taste in wine may be different to the famous Jerome Toper's; you may, therefore, find Jerome Toper's recommendations nondescript or puzzling. In that case, try the recommendations of someone else – Agatha Lippinglass, say, or Phil Tippler.

No, the real treachery of recommendations is that you may be led to think that unrecommended (or less highly marked) wines are less good than the recommended or highly marked wines, and therefore not worth trying. Sometimes, of course, such wines are mediocre and worthless; but there is, in all honesty, a vast middle-ground of wines of which it is very hard to say that one is better than another; they're simply different. Running your finger, metaphorically speaking, over all of the possible contours and outlines, dips and hollows, mounds and edges that you'll find in that vast middle-ground is, once again, the fun of wine. So don't feel hamstrung into buying only on recommendation, or following only high scores. Following your own nose is an enjoyable way forward, too.

Before we leave this subject, perhaps you might be interested to discover how recommendations are made – in my case, at any rate. Is there corruption at work?

Perhaps there is: I don't buy all the wines I recommend, and I don't get a chance to taste all the wines sold in Britain every year. Here's what happens.

With wines from high-street retailers and supermarkets, I try to attend as many tastings as possible, work my way through the wines, and then request samples of those that seem promising so that I can try them again – in order, most importantly, to drink them (rather than merely tasting them) at home with food. Judging wine by tasting it alone is unreliable, though sometimes unavoidable.

When I'm abroad visiting wine regions, where possible, the process is the same: request samples of wines which have impressed me to drink again at home with food before recommending them. Obviously this is not always possible – as when I am trying to assess the merits of a wide range of different wines prior to release (Bordeaux wines sold on an *en primeur* or pre-release basis, for example). Unhappily, I am aware that tips concerning, say, pre-release Bordeaux are probably the most important of all recommendations, since they concern expensive wines, which most of us cannot afford to make mistakes about.

The further failings and drawbacks of the system are obvious. Retailers can't show all the wines they offer, nor do all retailers organise tastings, and even if they did I wouldn't have enough time to go to them all. I'm not, therefore, truly sampling *everything* that's available. Retailers and importers also send out unrequested sample bottles of particular wines that they wish to promote, and careful study of my own recommendations, as well as those of others, reveals that these unrequested samples feature with more frequency and prominence than they probably merit. Retailers and importers, in other words, can manipulate journalists into recommending wines they wish them to. Which is another reason not to place too much trust in what we say.

94
Prices: double the price might not mean twice as good

There's one thing every reader (and, incidentally, the writer) of this book has in common. Not one of us likes to pay more than necessary for a bottle of wine.

But how much is necessary? As much and no more, I would argue, as you can easily afford.

This is not as stupid an answer as it might at first appear, for two reasons. The first is that one of wine's small miracles is that any thoughtful drinker can take as much pleasure in drinking a well made simple wine as he or she can in drinking the finest and most polished claret or burgundy. Indeed, since wine is subjectively appreciated and our enjoyment of it depends on mood and context, there are times when the simpler wine might provide more pleasure than the complex one: when you're tired, for example, or when your infant children are mountaineering over you, or when you are trying to make conversational headway in the noisy and distracting surroundings of a busy bar or restaurant. Good cheap wine is, at moments like that, great.

All good wine fascinates the mouth and the mind; the difference between say, the £5 and the £50 bottle, assuming both are true to their regional origins and well made, is one of character or personality, accompanied by finely graduated degrees of complexity, harmony and allusive power. The best is always rare; the rare is always expensive. What is never true, though, is that the £50 bottle will be ten times as good as the £5 one. It will be somewhat better: maybe 30 per cent better, maybe only five per cent better. Who can say for sure? There are bad expensive wines which may actually be worse than good cheap ones at a fraction of their price. By all means experiment with expensive wines, but do so as a lover or a gambler, rather than as an accountant. If you approach wine in search of value rather than beauty, poetry and singularity, it will always be hard to justify the prices of expensive wines.

What about the second reason for my apparently evasive answer as to how much one should spend on wine? It is this: the more you analyse the concept of 'good value', the more meaningless it becomes. Let's begin by assuming it means something like 'a sound product sold within the bottom third of the price band for that product', for example; it's hard to see how one can be any more specific than that. Millionaires might therefore talk of yachts or private jets as being good or bad value, something that those who empty dustbins or drive trucks for a living would find laughable. If you can afford a yacht or a jet, any wine which brings you pleasure is providing good value, since even £50 or £100 is an insignificant outlay. If you empty dustbins or drive trucks, no wine which costs £50 or £100 could ever provide good value, since that money is just too precious to you in other ways – buying loaves of bread to ensure you have enough energy for a day's work, or clothes to stop your children feeling cold on their walk to school. Where's the value, finally? It's relative, of course: we have to define it for ourselves.

That's why you should never spend more than you feel comfortable with on wine. Nor, contrariwise, should you spend less: those with comfortable incomes, large cars and automatic front gates who buy cheap wines are depriving themselves of profound and subtle pleasures and, despite their wealth, impoverishing their lives. Pity.

Part 6

The Table: Serving Wine

95 Don't serve white wine too cold

Our grand tour is complete now, so all that remains to do is to eat, drink and be merry. The easy bit, eh?

Quite. Just how you set about eating, drinking and being merry is up to you; I don't believe in rules and regulations when it comes to personal pleasures, nor would I impose them on myself at home. All the same, experience proves (as it usually does) that some stratagems work better than others. This last section, therefore, contains a few tips.

Let's start in the fridge. Cold, isn't it? Exactly: it's usually about 4°C or 5°C. Stick a good bottle of white burgundy in there the day before you want to drink it, get it out for your guests, open it, pour it, drink it – and you may well consider the wine a flop and your money wasted. The fact is that most fridges are far too cold for most white wines: white burgundy (and oaked Chardonnay in general) is best served at around 12°C, which is cool rather than cold. Overchilling richer styles of dry white wine closes them down and stifles their personalities like repressive parents deflating a child's imaginative games. If you don't have anywhere cool to place such wines (and outside temperatures in Britain are often ideal), then take them out of your fridge at least half an hour before serving.

Dry white wines, in general, are best served at around 10°C (so get them out of the fridge around 15 minutes before serving). Champagnes and sparkling wines should be served a little cooler again: straight from the fridge won't do any harm, though the second glass may be more communicative than the first; the same goes for fino and manzanilla sherry. The only wines which really do require serving almost iced, at 4°C–6°C, are dessert wines and sweet wines in general (including sweet fortified wines, if you fancy them chilled). Coolness then acts as a balancing factor, and the levels of sugar, alcohol and acidity are generally so high that even cold of this wintry an order cannot cramp their style.

96
Don't serve red wine too warm

I was with a friend recently, a wine merchant who lives in Italy. We stopped at a little roadside restaurant in the Tuscan woods for a late lunch of crostini and salami and prosciutto. "Some red wine, please" he asked the enormous Mama in charge of the establishment, "and an ice bucket." She waved her succulent finger at him. "Red wine's no good cold," she said. And that was that. She was not a woman to invite contradiction.

My friend and I smiled at each other. It wasn't, as it happened, too hot that day; indeed our consorts grew chilly in the breezy shade of our table under the acacia trees. If it had been midsummer, though, the temperature could quite easily have been 27°C or 29°C. And, *pace* Mama, that's too hot.

Red wine begins to fall to pieces at around 22°C. The acidity slides up and away from the fruit, which loses its poise and composure; the tannins head off in a different direction altogether. Over 25°C, and it begins to taste like soup. I remember this vividly since, when I first began drinking wine, a couple of decades ago, it was the custom, in the English countryside during the dark months, to put a bottle of red wine by a roaring fire or on a stove for an hour or so while one tossed back gin and tonic. After that, the wine *was* soup.

The ideal serving temperature for full-bodied red wines is around 20°C; and many mid- to full-bodied red wines (such as Bordeaux) taste better at 18°C. I'd guess that lots of you, just to put this into context, would be tempted to turn the central heating on if the temperature in your living room was only 18°; in our modern, globally warmed world, this is no longer 'room temperature' but relatively cool. Light red wines (such as most from the Loire or Beaujolais, which, although red in colour, actually have the structure and balance of white wines) are delicious when chilled to 14° or 15°C.

There's no great mystique about chilling red wine. If you're at home, stick it in the fridge for half an hour (or outside the back door in winter); if you're in a warm restaurant, ask for it to be put in an ice bucket. And good luck to you.

97
Breathing is a waste of time

As we discovered back in section 29, wines need air from time to time. One of those times is just before you drink it.

This is a truth vaguely and imperfectly understood – which has passed into drinking lore as the rule that wine, usually red, needs to 'breathe' for an hour or so. 'Breathing' means removing the capsule and cork and letting the wine stand in that state.

Think about it. What is the surface area of the wine exposed to air by such a process? It's no more than the circumference of a cork – almost nothing, in other words. And almost nothing will happen to the wine. This is why 'breathing' is a waste of time. Its real purpose, I'd say, is to act as a signal for host, hostess or guests that the point of no return has passed, that the bottle has been opened, that dinner is underway. That hour or so can then unfurl in happy anticipation of a liquid pleasure to come. It is, in other words, a sort of ritualised bacchic foreplay.

Ironically, many red wines and even some white wines would benefit from a true dose of air before they are served. This is particularly true of any wine, red or white, which you suspect is still young and some years away from its peak; it is also true of wines which may be over-reduced and suffering from 'bottle stink' (have another look at sections 29 and 45 if you've forgotten what this is). At home, I aerate almost all red wines (the only exception would be elderly reds, especially delicate ones like burgundy), and generally aerate white burgundy and white Rhône wines, too.

How? See the next section.

98 Use your decanter

We've got six or seven at home: simple, inexpensive, uncut. They're usually empty: it's a bad idea to leave any wine, even sherry and port, standing in a decanter for any length of time. I use ours to pour bottles of wine into, generally two to four hours before I serve them. (Occasionally, big, tough reds like Barolo might benefit from eight hours or more in a decanter.) That air will freshen almost all of them up, and in the case of youngish red wines will allow a little instant maturation to take place, unlocking their more interesting aromas, softening their tannins slightly and bringing their component parts together into harmony and wholeness. The same process can also help tight, taut, yet richly constituted dry whites, such as burgundies and Rhônes under a decade old, into articulacy. Indeed it's worth a try, on an experimental basis, with almost any wine. Cheap red wine, in a smoothly contoured plain glass decanter, looks indistinguishable from the finest red wine in the world, and white wines look appealing too, in decanters. They catch the light, and their green lemon and straw yellow colours deepen into a rich, fissured gold. Decanting provides what 'breathing' does not: exposure to air for all the wine in the bottle, with its attendant benefits. In the case of wines with sediment, too, it also provides a chance for you to pour the clear wine off the cloudy dregs. (How? Pour it into the decanter over a light source, and stop once you see cloudy wine leaving the bottle.)

You don't even need a decanter to decant wine, by the way. Pour the wine into a jug, then rinse out the original bottle and pour the wine back into that. No problem.

99 Red wine goes with fish

"OK, I'll try a bottle. But what would you recommend I serve it with?"

It's a familiar question to all of those who have worked (as I have) in a wine shop. Most wine lovers have enjoyed great wine and food experiences: meals where the two elements, solid and liquid, seemed not merely to like each other but to stand up, embrace and then dance round the table, forming a combination which was far better than the sum of the two parts. Lots of us then spend time trying to recreate that kind of magic – and, as often as not, failing. My own guess is that it has more to do with atmosphere and appetite than we suppose.

We also, of course, remember bad combinations. I've got some friends who had loved a claret I'd once brought them – so when my wife and I visited them a Christmas or two later I decided to bring another bottle of the same 1982 Bordeaux. We ate seafood paella. The wine was great. The seafood paella was great. The combination was grotesque. You live and learn.

Or perhaps I don't. My basic wine-and-food-matching philosophy is still to drink what I want and eat what I want, and hope that the combination works. In the main, it does, which is why I find a lot of food-and-wine rules both mystifying and stultifying. Each new food and wine equation is, it seems to me, far too complex ever to yield to any kind of predictive accuracy. I might say 'Bordeaux is great with lamb stew' – yet an over-aged, reedy Bordeaux will taste horrible with a lamb stew which contains too much salt and dried thyme. Whose Bordeaux, in other words? Whose stew? In the end, faced with the reality of an infinity of variables, you might as well go for what you fancy.

In general, I prefer red wine to white. At restaurants, I like to eat fish – so nine times out of ten I'll have red wine with my fish, and I'm generally very happy with the result. Claret and seafood paella may not go well together, but claret and grilled sea bass or roast cod is fine. In section 101 we'll consider a few adventurous combinations, while in section 100 we'll be looking at the most dangerous of liaisons. In this section, though, with our qualifications and cautions to hand, let's jog through the basic outlines of happy combining.

Beginning with meat. Red meat, red wine? Generally speaking, yes. The main thing to remember is the plainer and leaner the meat, the lighter the red wine should be. Save your monstrous 14.5% Shirazes or Châteauneufs for red meats in sauces, stews or pies, or with unctuous red meats like oxtail or lamb shank. If you like modest slices of boiled brisket, then light reds (burgundy or Beaujolais, for example, or global Pinot Noirs) are ideal.

White meats are perhaps the easiest of all foods to match with wine: chicken, turkey and pork go well with almost anything, red or white. For choice, light, tangy reds (from the South of France, perhaps) are best of all, and the richer whites (oaked Chardonnay, for example) are good too. Duck and goose are richer, so can take more assertive wines, particularly reds: this is the time to have a go with wines which may be high in both acidity and tannin like Barolo or Barbaresco. If you prefer white wines, try some with both acidity and sweetness, such as Vouvray from the Loire or Rieslings from Germany. Game birds and rabbit are good with reds from the Northern Rhône and Chianti. Please remember that these are only suggestions: if you want to drink your favourite Rioja with everything I've just mentioned then, hey, that'll be fine too.

What about fish? As I've already told you, I drink lots of red wines with fish and enjoy not only the wine and food but the combination, too. If I'm being sensible, I'd advise you to stick to lighter red wines, and chill them, too; but I'm not fond of being sensible ...

The classic fish partner, of course, is white wine. Low-personality whites like the Italian brigade and standard Chardonnay from anywhere will go with more or less anything, and classic French fish whites like Chablis and Sancerre are very good with Atlantic fish cooked plainly, or sauced deftly. For more exotic fish, try New Zealand's whites or Australian Riesling. Raw seafood (oysters and so on) adores very dry white wine; sometimes I think that's why Muscadet exists. One of the greatest meals of my life, though, was a basket of oysters, fresh bread and unsalted Normandy butter served, one hot spring day, with his own Blanc de Blancs Champagne by François Roland-Billecart of Billecart-Salmon. Chilled fino or manzanilla sherry, finally, are superb with the entire piscatorial spectrum.

Vegetables and salads give you lots of room for

experiment. Quite often, a tomato flavour dominates sauces in vegetable dishes, and low-acid, soft red wine (from Chile, say) goes well with this. New World white wines are a good starting point for salads. Gewürztraminer is the classic partner for Chinese foods, but plainer whites (from Italy or the Rhône) work well too. If you want to drink wine with hot and spicy food from the Indian or Thai traditions, you'll find wine can combine with these flavours surprisingly well: New World reds are good with Indian food, while France's less assertive whites (Bordeaux, Bergerac, Côtes de Gascogne) make creative foils to Thai food.

Cheese itself is not, contrary to popular opinion, best with red wine; sweet wines generally work better in practice, and my own favourite partner for cheese is port. Dessert wines, too, are paradoxically not necessarily best with dessert; I'd always recommend you try them on their own first. Many desserts make wines which taste sweet on their own suddenly taste disappointingly dry and austere. Again, a better general solution is fortified wine – try Malmsey Madeira, or some of Australia's superb Liqueur Muscats.

Above all, though: *don't worry about it*. If you're short of things to worry about, write to me and I'll give you a list. Food and wine matching won't feature.

100 The table of horrors

Generally, wine and food go well together; occasionally they don't. Here is a short account of notorious accident black spots on the wine-and-food highway.

Meals often begin with soups – and soup isn't well accompanied by wine. This is not so much due to its taste as its liquid texture. One of the purposes of wine with most foods is to act as a lubricant; with soup, it can't. Indeed the soup dilutes the wine. You might want to try a little glass of sherry or Madeira, since the strength of fortified wine gives it more of a handhold on soup's liquid evanescence, but nothing at all is probably best of all.

Fish? Salted, pickled and preserved fish can demolish wines comprehensively. Soused and salted herrings are best with chilled vodka, and the same is true of kippers. Other, chunkier smoked fish will put up with neutral Italian whites and some oaked wines, though the combination isn't great. Any dish in which vinegar or lemon juice plays a major part, such as dishes of winkles and cockles in Britain or dishes like ceviche elsewhere, will pose problems for wine. Capers are another peril, as are many proprietary sauces. Remember, too, that dishes customarily sprinkled with vinegar (like, famously, British fish and chips) don't actually need that vinegar if you're drinking wine with them. Wine 'cuts' through the stodge and the fat just as effectively, and a lot more palatably, than vinegar.

Meats of all sorts are generally very wine-friendly, though it's best not to waste good bottles on junk meat (all burgers except those you make yourself at home, chilli con carne, industrial sausages). Don't expect pickles and sauces to go particularly well with wine, either.

Vegetarians are often on the receiving end of a finger-wagging about how difficult it is to match wine with eggs and artichokes, quiches and omelettes, but most of this is exaggerated. If you're really looking for that perfect combination, then you'll probably stick to white wines, but I've drunk red wines with fried eggs on many occasions and always enjoyed myself.

Cheeses, I agree, are more difficult (on their

own; when used in cooking they are less problematic). One of the worst combinations of my life, indeed, was rosé Champagne served with unpasteurised Brie. The wine seemed to seal the cheese on to my tongue like a kind of lactic glue. In flavour terms, it made the cheese taste like scrapings from a barn owl's nest; the cheese then retaliated by making the wine resemble a cocktail of sulphuric acid and cranberry juice. Hard cheeses are generally more wine-friendly than soft or blue ones, but go carefully at all times and favour fortified and dessert wines over plain whites or reds.

Any wine other than the very sweetest is unpleasant when served with desserts or cakes, as anyone who's ever been to a wedding and 'enjoyed' Champagne with wedding cake will confirm. The sugar seems to drain all richness out of the wine, leaving even the amplest hollow and tart. Sweet fortified wines are, once again, the best solution – or an aromatic double espresso.

101 Give it a whirl

If you take an insouciant and piratical approach to wine-and-food matching, you're likely to discover some unusual matches which work well. Potentially there are hundreds of thousands of these: here are three, by way of inspiration or example, from my own notebook.

A fine, fresh mackerel is not only beautiful, with its silvery-blue iridescence, but it makes a tasty meal, too. It is, though, very oily, and that can be problematic for wines. I had a bottle of German Riesling open a month or two ago, a young Rheingau Spätlese – fresh, delicate, full of fruity acids yet slightly sweet, too, so with a few misgivings I launched into the combination. It was superb, with the wine's acids and sugars swimming gratefully into the fish's rich flesh.

What else? Oh yes: last summer's holiday on the Greek island of Paxos. Our apartment was self-catering; I bought, I remember, some small, elongated, very firm aubergines, and made them into a stew with garlic and tomatoes and herbs we'd picked up on the woodland path down to the beach. The books I've consulted generally suggest white wine with aubergines, but we drank the Naoussa of Boutari: a dark, tannic red with wonderfully complex flavours which reminded me of autumn leaves, dust and old leather. Maybe I drank finer wines with more skilfully prepared foods during 1997, but there was no combination that I enjoyed as much.

More recently, I found myself with some leftover white Rhône – very unctuous and rich, full of slippery glycerine, and a wine which managed to taste almost sweet while being at the same time technically dry. For supper, I'd bought some tiger prawns which I stir-fried with chopped garlic, ginger and chilli, then with peas, and finished it all with soy and a little shake of rice vinegar. It wasn't a classic combination (that would have been Gewürztraminer, Sauvignon Blanc or a white from Italy; and you might think it was a waste to serve highly flavoured food with a classy, nuanced white), yet it worked admirably, the bright flavours of the prawn dish sinking gratefully into the broad and succulent embrace of this passively assertive, haunting white wine.

So there we are: the end. An appropriate one, I hope, since we're lost in the pleasure of experiment, the enjoyment of diversity, the excitement of discovery. That's wine.

Further Reading

If you've enjoyed this introduction to the subject and want to learn more, here's where to go.

Magazines
Britain has two monthly wine magazines, available from newsagents and by subscription: *Decanter* and *WINE*. The American magazine *The Wine Spectator* is also available through some wine merchants and off-licences, and fine-wine enthusiasts are likely to find a subscription to Robert Parker's *Wine Advocate* useful (fax 001 410 357 4504 for more details).

Reference Books
A basic wine library should contain the following four reference books:
The World Atlas of Wine by Hugh Johnson (Mitchell Beazley)
The Story of Wine by Hugh Johnson (Mitchell Beazley)
The Wine Buyer's Guide by Robert Parker (Dorling Kindersley)
The Oxford Companion To Wine edited by Jancis Robinson M.W. (Oxford University Press).

Other good general books include:
Michael Broadbent's Winetasting (Mitchell Beazley)
Michael Broadbent's Wine Vintages (Mitchell Beazley)
Oz Clarke's New Classic Wines (Webster's/Mitchell Beazley)
Oz Clarke's Wine Atlas (Little, Brown)
Hugh Johnson's Pocket Wine Book (Mitchell Beazley)
Vines, Grapes and Wines by Jancis Robinson M. W. (Mitchell Beazley).

Index